COMPETITIVE OBEDIENCE
FOR WINNERS

Brian McGovern

RINGPRESS

RINGPRESS

Published by Ringpress Books Ltd,
PO Box 8, Lydney, Gloucestershire GL15 6YD.

Discounts available for bulk orders
Contact the Special Sales Manager at
the above address. Telephone 01594 563800.

First Published 1995.
© 1995 Brian McGovern and Ringpress Books.

ISBN 1 86054 035 X

Printed and bound in Singapore.
by Kyodo Printing Co.

CONTENTS

To Ria, my wife, and to Wimp (Sealight Wimp)
and Woolie (Colalbri Trickie Woo)
– with thanks to you all.

ACKNOWLEDGEMENTS

My thanks to Roelof Fermont for the photographs; Yvonne Ketelaar, Floor Renema, Lenie Kastelijin and Eric Kerkhof, for 'posing' for the photographs; and to Jeroen van Genk for the diagrams.

INTRODUCTION

I was fortunate to fall in love with dogs at a very early age, and ever since then they have played a major role in my life. When I was eight years old I first started 'collecting' dogs. My own family had a Border Collie called Prince, and later we had a mongrel from the local dog pound, which we called Dusty.

However, our neighbours always had a host of interesting and exciting dogs. The first that I remember was Winnie, a Greyhound, followed by Gyp, a German Shepherd Dog (or Alsatian as they were then called). I adopted Gyp, the Alsatian, and with Dusty, our own mongrel, I started my life with dogs. They were my constant companions, and I spent all my free time with them, playing in the large wooded area which bordered the housing estate where I lived. At this time, there was no thought of formal training – I did not even own a dog lead.

I first came into contact with Competitive Obedience in my late teens when I started attending a local dog training club with my two German Shepherd Dogs, Gyp and Kaiser. This club was primarily for pet dog training with a few competitive handlers. Like many other pet dog owners, I soon became smitten with the competition virus. I won my first beginners prize under Paula Ackery in the late sixties.

I moved to Holland in 1974, and once settled, I bought two German Shepherds, Ygor and Dacha. At that time there was no Competitive Obedience sport in Holland, and so I delved briefly into police dog training. Some time later I was invited to give lessons at a local pet dog training club which also ran classes for "Gedrag en Gehoorzaamheid", which can be loosely compared to Obedience.

In 1983 I thought of the idea of forming a national club to promote Competitive Obedience as per the English Kennel Club rules. Our first meeting was held in my sitting room and was attended by three people: Louise Mieras, who still competes occasionally, Rob Swarts, who was chairman of the Dutch Obedience Society for the first year before returning to his sport of police dog training, and myself.

In the first few years of the Dutch Obedience Society our main activities were organising competitions and arranging training weekends with guest instructors from England. Within a five year period we invited Charlie Wyant, Bing Bellamy, Bruce and Bronwyn Bartley,

*Jock vd Meywei
(Jock): Winner of the
Dutch Obedience
Championship 1987.*

Silvia and Roly Allebone, Karina Smith (now Griffiths), Herbie and Jennie Watson, Sue Potter, Silvia Bishop, John Higgens and Joanna Hill, and Sandy Wadhams. Many of these instructors were invited several times in the first few years, and it is because of these trainers, Louise Mieras, and others who invited these specialists, that Obedience in Holland has developed so quickly.

I have been lucky enough to win the Dutch Obedience Championships twice: in 1989 with Sealight Wimp (Wimpy), and in 1991 with Colalbri Trickie Woo (Woolie). Ria, my wife, won the Championships in 1987 with Jock vd Meywei (Jock). Our club members have also won the Championships: in 1990 and 1994 (Lenie Kastelijn with Whackie), and in 1992 and 1993 (Dominique Standaert with Ruffles). In 1992 and 1993 I was Reserve Champion with Woolie.

For this run of success we are indebted to all the trainers who have devoted time and energy to travel from England to teach in Holland. I would also like to mention Roy and Shelagh Page, and to thank them for all the hours spent 'dogging' round the kitchen table

Colalbri Trickie Woo (Woolie): Winner of the Dutch Obedience Championship 1991.

during their visits, and Ron and Silvia Mitchell because they are friends and 'kindred spirits'. Also thanks to the gang: Lenie, Monique, Mia, Guus, Dominique, and the rest, who have allowed me to experiment on them and thereby develop the methods described in this book.

Sandy Wadhams, more than any other person, has influenced my attitude towards play-training. Many of the principles and play techniques described in this book are adapted from Sandy's basic training. Sandy, in turn, names Charlie Wyant as her main influence, and so the art of training is passed on.....

I owe thanks to so many people who have influenced my training: Silvia and Roly who taught me to "cut the rubbish, keep it simple, and get on with it"; Charlie Wyant, who more than any other trainer has stamped his mark on modern Competitive Obedience, and many, many more. I would also like to thank Roelof Fermont for his willingness to devote so much time and effort to enhance this book with such wonderful photographs.

Last but not least I would like to thank Ria, my friend, wife and training partner, who has often had to put up with so much and has given me such support. We are lucky enough to share the same hobby which has allowed me to devote so much of my life to dogs. She is also a far better handler than I will ever be.

If I had to assess how much of this book and the techniques described in it were my own original concepts, then I would guess at less than twenty per cent. This book contains a collection of techniques that I have learnt from observing, listening to, and being taught by countless different dog trainers over the last thirty years. I believe that the most valuable aid to learning and expanding knowledge is the ability to observe and listen.

I enjoy teaching others as much as working my own dogs; I also believe that the ability to teach is improved by personal experience. Modern training methods are much more humane than those that were used when I first started training, and I make no apologies for adapting methods that were originally the concept of another. That is part of the learning. There is not one way to teach a dog, nor is there one method that will suit all handlers.

I have lost count of the times that I have presumed to take credit for developing a particular technique, only to attend a seminar or read a book and realise that my idea may not, after all, have been original. I cannot estimate how much of this book is 'mine', nor do I think it is an important issue. My intention is solely to describe how I train my dogs, and, hopefully, to help others to train theirs.

BRIAN McGOVERN,
AUTUMN 1994

Chapter One

PUPPY TRAINING

When I first started training dogs, most training clubs would not allow a puppy to attend training classes until it was at least six months old. Some trainers believed that twelve months was soon enough. Luckily, times and attitudes have changed, and it is now generally accepted that the first few months of a dog's life are the most important and valuable time to begin training. A puppy is constantly learning each day and will do so regardless of whether we are intentionally teaching him or not. Puppies also learn very quickly because they have no preconceived opinion of a particular situation. We can therefore make use of the pup's open-mindedness to lay the basis for our future Champions.

There is so much we can teach a young puppy that it would take a separate book to cover everything. Therefore, this chapter is restricted to information related to teaching the exercises and preparing the puppy for the lessons to be taught in Competitive Obedience training. This does not imply that competition training should take precedence over pet dog training – they should go hand in hand. It is simply because this book is about Competitive Obedience training. My competition dogs are, first and foremost, obedient pet dogs.

OPPORTUNITY TRAINING
Initially, I prefer to introduce a puppy to training in such a way that the puppy never realises that he is being trained. I call this 'opportunity training'. I coax the puppy into a particular situation, and *if* I get the hoped for-reaction, I give the activity a name, which will later become the formal command for that exercise. An example will clarify this: I take the puppy into the garden and let him run free. I will then do something, such as play with a toy, or clap my hands and make interesting noises to get the puppy's attention. If he looks up at me, I back away from him to encourage him to come to me. If the puppy responds, I introduce the Recall command, together with lots of praise, while the puppy is running to me. If the puppy decides not to come, I do not give the command. The command will only be given if the puppy is already doing what is required of him.

In this way, we can teach the puppy the Watch, Sit, Down, Stand, Recall, Heel position, Present, Sendaway and Scent commands before he is three months old. More importantly, by the use of 'opportunity training', the puppy will learn that co-operating leads to a reward.

In this way, we can develop the will to please. I use food rewards for this initial training in preference to play, as play needs preparatory work to ensure that the puppy does not resent giving up his toy reward, whereas with food rewards this is not the case.

I give the puppy the command for a particular exercise about one hundred times while he is already doing what I want, before I attempt to change the timing. So, initially, the sequence is: action, command, then reward, which after a hundred repetitions will be changed to: command, (re)action, reward. Some puppies cotton on much quicker than others, but I have found that a hundred repetitions is enough for even the slowest learner.

Once the sequence has been altered to command, reaction, and reward, we must introduce the three phases of reward (see Chapter Two: Motivation and Reward) to ensure that the puppy will react to the verbal command. Each time I introduce a new exercise, I hold the food reward in a way that will coax the puppy to react in the required way. It is important to be aware that this hand movement, while crucial in getting the required reaction, may become *the* command to the puppy. Therefore, you may have to wean the puppy off this 'command' once he is confident in the exercise.

All initial training should be done either sitting on the ground, or kneeling down with both knees on the ground. This makes contact with the puppy so much easier.

ATTENTION TRAINING
Attention training is such an important topic that I have devoted a separate chapter to it (see Chapter Three: Attention Training). The basic method for teaching attention is the same for both a puppy and an adult dog. However, a puppy is naturally less independent than an (untrained) adult, and more interested in everything that we do.

As with new commands, I wait until the puppy is doing what I want before giving the command. With the use of toys or a tidbit, I attract the pup's attention, and while he is watching in anticipation of getting his reward, I introduce the command "Watch". The attention span of a young puppy is very short, so it would be a mistake to insist that the pup keeps watching for more than a second or two. The puppy must be rewarded the instant you get the correct response.

Sit or kneel on the ground with four or five pieces of food in your hand. Show the puppy the food and give him a piece. Once he has eaten it, he will look at you hoping for another piece. This is the moment to introduce the Watch command, with lots of praise, and give him another piece of food. Repeat this until all five pieces have been given. Do not make the puppy wait for more than a second or two between each reward. The whole training session should take only ten or fifteen seconds. All we want to do is to give the Watch command while the puppy is watching. Teaching the puppy to watch, and keep watching, comes much later (see Chapter Three).

The Watch command can also be introduced during play. Sit or kneel on the ground and encourage the puppy to play with a toy. Gently ease the toy out of the pup's mouth, and hold it in plain view in your hand at chest level. If the puppy attempts to snatch the toy back, do not correct him, just hold the toy out of his reach. Once the puppy realises that he cannot get the toy, he will look at you to 'beg' you to play. As he does so, introduce the Watch command, praise, and then reward by giving the puppy his toy. In this way, the puppy will learn that you dictate the conditions of play, and he will learn to look at you for permission to do so. The drawback with this method is that the inexperienced handler often fails to develop the play, so that the puppy is playing with him as opposed to in competition against him. Correct play often takes a while to develop, which is why I prefer food-training with very young puppies, leaving play for what it is – a fun-time, and a good way of finishing off each training session. Once play has been developed, you can choose either food or play as your method of reward.

THE SIT

Kneel on the ground with the puppy on the lead, held in the left hand. In your right hand, hold a tidbit, and allow the puppy to sniff it. Move the food up and over the puppy's head, just out of his reach. The puppy will probably jump up and move about in an attempt to reach the food. Encourage (without praising) the puppy with your voice, making sure that he cannot get the reward. Do not attempt to command or place the puppy into the Sit, just be patient. Once the puppy realises that he cannot reach the food, he will go into the Sit, simply because it is easier to look up from the Sit than it is from the Stand. Immediately give the command "Sit" followed by lots of verbal praise, and then the food reward. Do not try to keep the puppy in the Sit – we are teaching the Sit, not the Sit-stay. The puppy need only sit long enough to get the food reward, which follows the verbal praise.

*Teaching
the Sit*

*Encourage your
puppy to pay
attention by
allowing him to
sniff the tidbit,
held in your
hand.*

Move your hand above the puppy's head. The puppy will go into the Sit as it is easier to look up at the tidbit from this position. Praise and give the Sit command only once the puppy is sitting.

It may take some time to get the first Sit, which will be more or less accidental, but I have never known a puppy to take more than a minute or two to work it out. Once the first Sit, with the accompanying praise and reward has been achieved, the second Sit will take much less time – usually only a few seconds – and by the end of the first training session the puppy will be sitting immediately the food is held above his head. Repeat the Sit exercise nine or ten times, and then end the training session.

One fault that often creeps in with this method is that the puppy sits and then lifts his front legs off the ground as he gets the reward. If this happens, just lift the reward out of reach until the puppy goes back into the Sit. This may happen several times before the puppy learns to keep all four feet on the ground. Occasionally a puppy will get frustrated because he does not get the reward immediately, and so he loses interest. If this happens, give him the food anyway. The puppy has not been given a command, so you are not rewarding the dog for failing to react.

The puppy that shows no interest in the food is a different matter altogether. In this situation, we must first determine the reason for the lack of interest. Are you using soft, wet food? Has the puppy just been fed? Are you using the same type of food that he gets at meal times? It is essential to remember that a reward must be something the puppy really *wants*, in order to avoid this problem.

Teaching the Down

Kneel on the ground and show your puppy the tidbit. Place the food on the ground and cover it with your hand. The puppy will go into the Down when attempting to get at the food. At this moment, give the command "Down".

THE DOWN

Kneel on the ground with the puppy on the lead, and with food in your right hand, as when teaching the Sit exercise. Show the puppy the food, and then place the food on the ground and cover the food, using your open hand as an umbrella to prevent the puppy from getting it. As with the Sit, the puppy will attempt various ways of getting the food. He can smell the food but he cannot see it, so he will try to force your hand out of the way with his nose to get at it.

The pup will soon realise that it is much easier to attempt this from the Down. The moment he lies down, pick up the food, introduce the command "Down", praise verbally and reward with the tidbit, making sure that the food is given while the puppy is in the Down. If you raise your hand from the ground to give the tidbit, this will encourage the puppy to go to the Sit, so make sure the hand stays low. As with the Sit exercise, the first time will be the most difficult. Repeat the exercise ten times, and then finish the training session. Occasionally, a puppy will try to dig the reward out from under your hand by scratching with his paws, which can be very painful. If this happens, do not scold the puppy – this will only teach him to avoid the hand altogether. With this sort of puppy, it is preferable to use another method.

Sit on the ground, with your left leg tucked under your bottom and your right leg stretched out, with the knee bent, to form a bridge. Place the puppy on the left side of your outstretched right leg, and place your right hand, containing the tidbit, under the bridge of the knee from the right side. As the puppy tries to get the tidbit, draw your hand back under the bridge. The puppy will try to follow the tidbit, and he must lie down in order to do so. As the puppy lies down, give the command "Down", verbal praise, and reward.

The drawback with this method is that the puppy moves forward into the Down, whereas the other method encourages a backward movement. We do not want to encourage forward movement, as this will conflict with teaching Distant Control later on. Therefore, once the puppy has got the idea and is going into the Down, place the food on the ground under your leg, and cover it with your hand, as in the first method. Do this several times, and then attempt the first method in full. Hopefully, you will find that the dog no longer scratches at your hand, but now lies down to get the reward.

THE STAND

This exercise is preferably taught from the Sit, and to avoid confusion it should only be introduced once the puppy is happy and confident in the Sit. Kneel on the ground with the lead and tidbit in the hand, as when teaching the Sit and the Down. Show the puppy the

Teaching
the Stand

Start with your puppy in the Sit and show him the tidbit. As the puppy tries to take it, move your hand under his chin. The puppy, attempting to get the food, will tuck his head into his chest and arch his back, going into the Stand. The hand should be kept still to discourage forward movement.

food, and as he tries to take it move your hand under his chin and back towards his throat. This will make the puppy tuck his head into his chest in an attempt to get the reward. His back will arch as he goes into the Stand, while at the same time he will move backwards to get the reward. As the puppy stands, give the command, verbal praise, and then the reward. Repeat ten times and finish the training session.

The Stand is the most difficult of the three positions to teach, and the positioning of the hand under the chin must be exactly right for it to succeed. Sometimes a puppy will just roll over into the Down if the hand is not positioned correctly. If this happens, just offer the food to the puppy in the Sit and draw the hand slightly forward. The moment the puppy raises his back-end into the Stand to reach for the food, place it under the chin, as described, to get backward movement. Two or three times should be enough for the puppy to get the idea, and then you can revert to placing the food under the chin without the forward movement.

THE RECALL
The basis of a good Recall can be taught long before a puppy can sit and wait to be called.

With the help of someone to hold the dog, the Recall can be introduced in a similar way to the Sit, Down and Stand. Ask the helper to hold the dog by the collar, walk a few yards away, and sit on the ground with your legs spread out in front of you to form a 'V'. Attract the puppy's attention, and then show him his reward by holding both hands out in front of

Teaching the Recall

With a helper holding the puppy, walk a short distance away and kneel, or sit, on the ground, with your thighs forming a 'V' to guide the puppy. Give the Come command as the puppy runs to you.

you. Once you have the attention, tell the helper to release the puppy, and encourage the pup to run to you. As he is running towards you, introduce the Recall command – "Come" – together with lots of praise to excite the puppy. As the puppy reaches you, draw your hands into your body so that he comes between your legs, which are acting as a funnel. Raise your hands to your chest so that the puppy comes into contact with your body. Do not attempt to get the puppy to sit – that comes much later.

Now, ask the helper to come and collect the pup and repeat the exercise several times. As the helper is taking the puppy away, try to keep the pup's attention and make yourself interesting so that the puppy would rather stay with you. This will make him even keener to come the next time.

It is also possible to double the amount of Recalls taught in any one session if the helper is someone that the puppy knows well. All you have to do is alternate being helper and caller. Start off as previously explained, and then once the helper has released the puppy, he can sit on the ground while you hold the puppy, and he can call the puppy back. The puppy will soon learn to quickly run to and fro, and will find it all great fun.

SENDAWAY

There are several ways of introducing the Sendaway command. One of the easiest ways is to incorporate the command between two callers, as described in the Recall. The helper holding the puppy can give the Sendaway command – "Away" – as the puppy is released. Once the puppy is moving, the caller gives the Recall command. In this way, two exercises are being taught simultaneously. Prior to releasing the puppy and giving the Sendaway command, the helper can also introduce the command "Look straight" while the puppy is looking at the caller.

Mealtimes are always a valuable training period, and the ideal time to teach the Sendaway. Let the puppy jump around and watch you prepare his meal. Pick the puppy up or restrain him by his collar, and place his food bowl on the ground. Lead the puppy a few yards away, and then release him to run to his food bowl. As he sets off, give him the Sendaway command. The command "Look straight" may also be introduced, but only if the puppy is looking at his food bowl. Later on, the food bowl can be used outside in the garden, with a tidbit in it, to expand the basic lesson.

Never demand a Down at the end of the Sendaway. All that is required, at this stage of training, is that the puppy associates the command with running in a straight line to a certain place, and is rewarded for doing so.

THE PRESENT

The Present should only be introduced once the puppy is happily sitting on command. Depending on the size of the puppy, either sit on the ground with your legs in a 'V', or kneel down with your bottom resting on your heels, with your thighs apart, so that the puppy can come in between to Present. Very large puppies will not fit in between your legs in this position, and so this step must be left out and a chair should be used, as explained in Chapter Eight.

First, let the puppy walk round at the end of a loose lead, and attract his attention with the reward held in both hands. Stretch your arms out, and encourage the puppy to take the food. As he attempts to do this, bring your arms into your groin – to get the puppy in close – and then up to your chest – to encourage the Sit. As the puppy comes into the Present, give him the Sit command.

The action of raising your hands combined with the Sit command, is very similar to the technique used in teaching the Sit, and it should result in a quick Sit. Your legs will ensure that the puppy sits straight. If the puppy refuses to sit, take your hands up and over his head, as in teaching the Sit. Do not give another command, just wait until the puppy sits before praising and rewarding. In this way, the puppy is called into the Present without having to do a Recall first. The pup can be anywhere within a 180 degree radius within arm's length, and so will learn to come in between the legs and present.

Teaching the Recall Present

Kneel on the ground with your thighs forming a 'V'. Use a tidbit, held in both hands, to attract the puppy's attention. As the puppy comes into the Present, raise both arms to your chest and give the Sit command. The 'V' formed by your legs will guide the puppy in and make him sit straight. With very large dogs or puppies, a stool or chair can be used instead of kneeling on the ground.

SITTING AT HEEL

Kneel on the ground with the puppy on the lead, held in your right hand. Tempt the puppy with food held in your left hand, and as the puppy tries to take the food, guide him with the left hand back behind you, and then forward again into the Heel position. If the puppy is happy and confident in the Sit, give him the Sit command. Once he is sitting in the Heel position, introduce him to the command for this exercise – "Heel" – praise and reward him.

Do not insist on a perfectly straight Sit. All you want is the dog to understand that the command means go and sit at the left side, and to do so happily. Precision will come later. If the puppy has been taught a correct Sit, he will, as often as not, sit correctly anyway. If the Sit exercise has not been developed, then this exercise can still be taught without giving the command to sit. Just let the puppy stand in the Heel position.

SCENT DISCRIMINATION

Introducing the puppy to Scent Discrimination can be done during play periods, and it should be lots of fun.

USING TOYS

Sit on the floor and play with the puppy, using one of his favourite toys. Get the puppy in front of you and show him the toy, and then quickly reach round behind you and place the toy on the floor. Bring your hand back around to the front, and show the puppy that you do not have the toy in your hands. Encourage the puppy to look for the toy by saying something like: "Where is it, then?" or "Where's your toy gone?" and as he starts to look for it, introduce the command to find – "Find" or "Seek". If the puppy does not understand and will not attempt to search, just reach around and pick up the toy, then break off into play. It may take several repetitions before the puppy gets the idea.

Once the pup does understand and is running around your back to look for his toy, try placing the toy behind you. As the puppy goes around to find it, bring it back in front from the opposite side that the puppy has chosen, and place it under one of your legs. Keep encouraging the puppy to "Find" while he is searching. By alternately placing the toy behind you and under your legs, the puppy will learn to use his eyes and nose to look for his toy.

It should now be possible to start to hide the toy behind the leg of a table or some other piece of furniture, or half hidden under a mat, and encourage the puppy to find his toy in lots of different places. Gradually place the toy completely out of sight, so that the puppy will naturally start to use his nose if he cannot find it with his eyes. Within a few weeks it should be possible to hide the toy in another room before taking the puppy into the room and letting him search for his toy.

Do not use the same toy every time, but each time a new toy is introduced, the puppy should play with it first. If you are the untidy type that leaves toys lying around and the puppy brings the 'wrong' toy back, just praise him and tidy up next time.

USING FOOD

Another method of introducing the puppy to Scent is with the use of tidbits. Take a scent cloth and a piece of food and show the puppy the food. Then place the food in the cloth, and tie a knot in the cloth with the food inside. Let the puppy sniff the cloth, then untie the knot and give the puppy the reward. Repeat this a few times, and then place the cloth on the floor with a piece of food in it. The moment the puppy sniffs the cloth, introduce the Scent command – "Find" or "Seek"– praise him, untie the knot and give him the food. Once the puppy understands the object of the exercise, you can 'tease' him with the knotted cloth containing the food, and then place it behind your back as described with the play method. From then on, the method is the same as when using a toy.

Whether you are using a toy or food, do not demand that the puppy brings the article back to you. When he goes off to search, go with him and praise him for looking and finding the article, not for retrieving it.

PRIORITIES

It should now be clear that even very young puppies can be taught a great deal. With a correct attitude and a good technique, a puppy can be introduced to most of the exercises that will be taught later on. However, we must remember at all times that the priority in puppy training is confidence-building and bonding through use of these exercises, not the exercises as such. All training sessions should be relaxed and fun, and if the puppy manages to learn a particular command this should be viewed as a bonus. In this way, the puppy will be prepared to be responsive and willing to be taught the formal exercises when the time comes.

Chapter Two

MOTIVATION AND REWARD

STIMULATION

Prior to actually starting to train your dog, it is important to decide how you are going to motivate and reward the dog for undertaking an activity that he would not normally choose to do. The handler must be able to immediately communicate to the dog that he is doing what is required of him, and to reward him for a job well done. It would be wonderful if the dog would accept a pat on the head and a verbal "good boy" as reward enough for all the hard work. Unfortunately, verbal praise is not usually enough reward, and so we need the constant reinforcement of play or food (or both) to support and give value to our verbal praise. At the same time, the handler must be aware of both the advantages and disadvantages of food and play-training. Pavlovian type conditioning, where the dog works purely for his reward, does little or nothing towards building up the relationship between dog and handler that is essential for Competitive Obedience.

The correct use of food and play as a support and aid to verbal praise will teach the dog to recognise and value the handler's voice and touch, and accept them as praise and encouragement, while at the same time establishing a bond with the dog and improving the mutual relationship. There are, I presume, a few gifted trainers with so much natural ability that they can communicate and bond with their dogs without the support of food or toys. However, most of us fall short of this perfection and therefore have to work hard to achieve the same goal. A thorough understanding of the principles, techniques, advantages and shortfalls of food and play-training is essential in order to obtain maximum benefit from their use.

CHOOSING A METHOD

It would be wrong to insist that every trainer must play-train or food-train their dog. It would be equally incorrect to say that a handler must use either one or the other. The aim is to motivate a dog to willingly carry out a command and to reward him for doing so. Logically speaking, it would therefore be wrong to use play as a reward for a dog who does not enjoy playing. Equally, there is no point in offering a food reward to a dog who is not interested in food. Both types of dog exist.

Lots of praise, together with food or play will motivate your dog to produce his best work. This seven-month-old Standard Schnauzer is already focusing all attention on the handler

I, personally, prefer to play-train my dogs. However, I encourage the majority of my beginner pupils to start off with food-training. I do this because I find that food-training is easier to teach and understand, while play-training needs more insight and understanding, which is often beyond the capabilities of most beginner handlers. This does not mean that beginner handlers are not encouraged to play with their dogs. There are play periods in every lesson, but they are playing just for the fun of play, and not specifically play-training.

The techniques I use can, with only slight adaptation, be used for either food or play-training, and it is quite normal to see half of my pupils in one class using food while the other half are play-training. Many of my pupils use both methods. To reward a dog (or human), and to motivate him to carry out an activity, we must simply offer something that *he* wants, not something that we think is a reward but which means little or nothing to him. The reward should also be something that the handler feels comfortable with and believes in. So many handlers do not enjoy playing with their dogs, but believe that they must do it because everyone else does. Equally wrong is the handler who relies solely on food to motivate their dog, because they will not make the effort to be active and positive in their training.

FOOD-TRAINING

ADVANTAGES
Food-training is systematic and is easy for the beginner to understand. The instructor has the advantage that the pupil can be sent home with a specific amount of homework to do. There are very few dogs who will not react to food-training, simply because *all* dogs eat. Occasionally, a handler will say that their dog is not motivated by food, only to find that this is not the case. If the dog is hungry and is offered the right type of food as reward, all dogs can be food-trained. The technique of rewarding the dog with food is simple to learn. Initial progress with food-training is faster than with play-training. Resentment in association with reward is non-existent because the dog may keep the food reward, whereas he must give the toy reward back.

DISADVANTAGES
If wrongly used, a handler can end up with a dog that sees food as the *only* motivation to work. The handler needs to use less energy and effort to persuade the dog to carry out a command than with play, resulting in the food becoming so important that it is indispensable. The food is no longer an aid that supports the verbal praise, but the *only* reward. With certain types of dog, daily mealtimes have to be scheduled around the training, which can restrict the 'any time, anywhere' type of trainer.

It should be noted that the disadvantages mentioned here are caused by the incorrect use of food.

PLAY-TRAINING

ADVANTAGES
Play is natural to all puppies, and it plays an important role in deciding who is who within the family group. It is the ideal way of establishing, without negative force, who is going to be the pack leader. By constantly playing with your dog, you will become the centre of his world and the most important thing in his life. By the correct use of play, we can give a submissive puppy confidence, and teach a bossy puppy who is in charge. Your dog will learn to enjoy being spoken to, he will learn to understand your tone of voice, and will enjoy being touched and handled. The handler can recognise a dog's state of mind by understanding that if he is unsure or frightened he will not play, and if he is willing to play he is relaxed enough to be trained. Perhaps most important of all, play is lots of fun.

DISADVANTAGES

Not all adult dogs want to play, and not all handlers want to either (although both can be taught). Playing with a dog and play-training are two different things. Play-training needs expert guidance for the beginner handler, and insight – which the beginner handler has to be taught. Play can often get out of hand and become a battle of wills between dog and handler. This is especially important when using toys. A playful tug-of-war can develop into a test of strength and character if you do not recognise the warning signs. To develop play into a tool that can be used as motivation and a reward in training can take many months, therefore initial progress can be slow. The difference between the dog playing *with* you, and not *against* you in 'playful' competition, is difficult to recognise.

Once play has been developed, training starts without the dog even realising that he is being trained; he should not see any difference between play and work. This means that the handler must be proficient in the technique to be used so that it is done spontaneously, and this obviously restricts play-training for the novice handler. Many handlers do not know where to draw the line. They take play-training to an extreme, resulting in the dog being OTT (over the top) and then the handler has to resort to disciplining the dog prior to competing.

Perhaps the most common mistake seen today is the handler who excites the dog by letting him tug on the lead or his toy for ten minutes, has a fight to get the dog to release the toy, then does ten minutes of formal Heelwork, only to finish off with another ten minutes of tugging – and then he tells everyone that he play-trains his dog.

USING FOOD

Using food (or play) to motivate and reward a dog is simple, as long as you bear in mind that it is an aid to verbal and physical rewards. It is important to guard against the dog mistakenly making the wrong association. If you give the dog a Sit command and reward him with a tidbit for sitting, the dog will learn to sit and will do so happily. If you tell the dog to sit, praise him for sitting, and reinforce verbal praise with a tidbit, the dog will learn to sit and will learn to recognise your voice as praise. Likewise, if you always hold the tidbit in sight when you command the dog to sit, the dog can make the wrong association and think that he only has to sit when he sees the food. These two examples illustrate the most common mistakes made when food-training.

THE THREE PHASES

Initially, food should always follow verbal encouragement and praise so that later on, the dog will accept verbal praise as the reward. Food should also be used in three phases: in sight, in the hand but out of sight, and in the pocket (or container). Using the Sit exercise as an example: show the dog the food, command him to sit, and reward with praise, followed by the food reward. Repeat this several times. Then, with the food in the hand but out of sight, command the dog to sit. When the dog sits, produce the food, and give this to the dog after verbal praise. Next, with empty hands, tell the dog to sit and praise him for doing so verbally, then take the food out of the pocket and give it to him. This (simplified) example is how I use food. In this way, we reduce the risk that the dog will only work for visible food

Food rewards should always be used in conjunction with physical and verbal rewards.

rewards, while at the same time establishing the value and meaning of verbal praise. On a technical note, I would normally release the dog from the Sit after the voice praise, but before the food reward.

The three phases of food reward are taught and repeated in each step of each exercise. It would be wrong to teach the first five steps of Heelwork using only phase one of food reward, and then try to remove the visible reward. The longer the reward is in sight, the greater the risk that the dog will misunderstand and perhaps see the visible reward as the command. I have found that using all three phases of food-training, while teaching the three basic Attention and five basic Heelwork steps, gives the dog enough time to understand that the reward is always there, even if he cannot see it. Thereafter the food reward can be left out of sight (phase three) while teaching further steps.

The command "Sit" is reinforced with verbal praise and a food reward.

When first introducing food, the dog must be taught three commands:
1. "Training" – which means training has started.
2. "Take it" – which means the dog can take his food reward.
3. "Finished" – which releases the dog from training.

PLAY-TRAINING

Before using play as motivation and reward to train your dog, it is important to first establish the ground rules. Similar to the commands in food-training, the dog must learn that there are four basic commands (compared to three in food-training) in play. These are:
1. "Training" – which means you are training and from that moment on the dog must at all times pay attention.
2. "Take it" – which means the dog may have the toy.
3. "Leave it" – the command that the dog must immediately and willingly release the toy.
4. "We are finished" – which tells the dog that training is over and releases him from

By constantly playing with your dog, you will become the centre of his world.

watching. These four commands, and what they mean, must be understood by the dog and firmly established before you can actually start to teach an exercise. In particular, the commands "Take it" and "Leave it" must be understood. The dog must only take the toy when told to do so. You must be able to control the play, and not be physically restricted or prevented from giving verbal encouragement because the dog keeps trying to snatch the toy. You must be able to 'tease' the dog and excite him, keeping his complete attention, but with the dog accepting that you are in control and he can take the toy only when given the command to do so. The same principle applies to the command "Leave it". The dog must immediately, and willingly, release the toy on command, without any resentment. These two commands establish your position as pack leader, and until such time that the dog accepts your leadership and understands the rules of the game, you cannot use play as a training tool.

Insight and experience in reading the dog are imperative in developing the play routine prior to using play as a training aid. You must be able to read the dog's reactions and alter

It is important to be able to read your dog's reactions and alter the play routine accordingly.

the play content accordingly. A boisterous, confident dog will probably try to take over the play. Therefore, this type of dog must not be allowed to 'win' or play tug-of-war as often as a dog with a more pliable character. On the other hand, a less assured dog can be allowed to 'win' more often to give him confidence. In this way, you must first shape the character of the dog during play, before utilising the play in training. This can take many months with certain types of dog.

In play-training, the same three phases are used as in food-training: toy in sight, toy in the hand but out of sight, and toy out of sight (e.g. in the pocket). The only exception to this would be if you are using the lead as a toy, in which case phase three would be omitted, as all training is done on lead. I use the lead as one of the many different toys in play-training. The lead is the only toy that can be taken into the ring.

Once the ground rules have been established, the first three steps of Attention training and the first five steps of Heelwork can be taught, by which time the dog will understand that his reward will come, even if he cannot see it. It is of paramount importance that, initially, the dog sees no difference between playing and training. The handler's attitude, verbal encouragement and body language must stay exactly the same in play or work. If not, the dog may realise that play and work are two separate entities, and you will have failed in your intention to play-train.

In the following chapters, I have referred to food as motivation and reward when describing the methods I use to teach the exercises. This does not imply a preference for food on my part, but is merely to avoid repetition and possible confusion. The principle is the same; it is a matter of deciding which method is best suited to the individual dog and handler. If the relevant ground rules are observed, and the advantages and disadvantages fully understood, it is a question of personal preference.

Chapter Three

ATTENTION TRAINING

The one thing that all trainers seem to agree upon is that Attention training is the first thing that must be taught to a dog. In fact, I believe that it is impossible to teach a dog anything until he has been taught to give complete and undivided attention. Unfortunately, it is the one exercise that many people find the most difficult to teach. However, if the basic principles of training are understood, there is no reason why there should be any major problems in teaching a dog to pay attention.

WHERE TO TRAIN?
The first thing you need to decide is where you are going to do your initial training. You must select a place that is familiar to the dog, where he feels relaxed, and there must be no distractions whatsoever. An ideal place is a spare room at home, or in the garage. Less suitable, but a good second choice, is a quiet corner of the garden. However, I prefer to train indoors, where I can control the distraction level. When teaching all exercises, even to an advanced dog, distractions should be nil. A dog (or person) cannot concentrate or learn when the attention is constantly distracted. An exercise should only be conducted under these conditions once the dog has been taught, and is confident, with the exercise.

I believe that the worst place to teach a dog a new exercise is at a training club. Training clubs are where the handler is taught how to train his dog, and the lessons that he learns there should be put into practice at home, without distraction. I cannot emphasise too strongly the importance of choosing the right training area. Attention training is the first introduction to formal training, and if you start by repeatedly correcting the dog because he is distracted, there is a good chance that he will associate training with correction and stress. If you approach Attention training in the right way, there should be no need for correction. The choice of training area is therefore crucial to success.

Teaching a dog to happily pay attention without distractions should only take two or three weeks. Before starting training, you should have already decided whether you will be using food or play for motivation and reward. As mentioned earlier, I will refer to food as the reward, highlighting differences in technique when play is used, where appropriate.

ATTENTION ON THE MOVE

WEEK ONE
Put your dog on the lead and take him into the training area. You should have prepared fifteen to twenty pieces of food, and you proceed to feed the dog with the tidbits. This should only take a minute or two, which means that the dog will receive a piece of food every three or four seconds. Each time that you give the dog a piece of food you will do several things:

1. Show the dog the food, which is held in your hand, and talk in an exciting voice which will encourage him to keep watching you. This tone of voice will be used in further training to encourage the dog while he is working.

Attention on the move

Show your dog a food reward, and talk in an exciting voice to keep attention focused on you.

2. As you give the food, praise in the tone of voice that will tell the dog that he has carried out a command correctly. Many handlers have difficulty in differentiating between the 'encouragement' and 'reward' tone of voice. If I find a handler with this problem, I suggest using a key word such a "Yes" or "That's it" to tell a dog that he has reacted correctly. This leaves all other voice-use as encouragement praise. An example will clarify this:

If a dog is lagging in Heelwork and the handler tries to motivate him into the correct Heelwork position by telling him he is a "good boy", the dog may believe that the handler wants him to lag because in the other exercises the handler used "good boy" as praise to tell him that he was correct. By using a key word when the dog is working correctly this confusion can be avoided.

3. While the dog is looking up in anticipation of receiving a tidbit, introduce the Attention command, e.g. "Watch", that will be used for attention in all further training.

4. Give an occasional gentle tug on the lead while simultaneously praising with both voice and a food reward. This will teach the dog that a tug on the lead is not a correction.

5. Take a step or two to the left or right, perhaps even slowly turning away, so that the dog follows to keep you in sight.

Once all the food has been given, tell the dog that training is finished by giving the command "OK", "That's it" or such like, and end the training session. This lesson should be repeated for the first week, preferably two or three times per day, if possible. It only takes a minute or two, so this should be feasible. During the first week, you do not want to correct the dog at all so if he should look away, just tempt him back by placing food under his nose. By the end of the first week, the dog should be excited the moment that he enters the training area. Let's face it, he goes in there, gets lots of praise and food, and nothing is demanded of him. Any normal dog, if he could speak, would tell you that it's fun!

WEEK TWO

In the second week, continue as before with one or two subtle changes. Extend the interval between giving each piece of food so that there can be up to ten seconds between each reward, while encouraging and praising the dog with your voice. You can also remove the visual aid of the food reward by giving half the food as you did in week one, and then hiding some of the food in the palm of the other hand. It is important to keep on talking to the dog just as you did when he could see the food. There are two possible things that can happen next:

1. The dog will keep on paying attention, in which case praise him, give the Attention command, and reward with the 'hidden' food.

2. Alternatively, the dog will look away because the visual aid of the food reward has been removed. If this happens, firmly, but without frightening the dog, call his name and give him a tug on the lead. The moment you get his attention back, praise him, give the Attention command, reward with food and then release him.

If the first week's work has been thoroughly taught, I would not expect to have to correct the dog at all, or at most, only once or twice. If you find that the dog tries to look away more than once or twice, stop training and try to think about what is going wrong. Are there distractions? Are you being interesting enough? Try to find the answer before continuing training. Whatever the reason, do not carry on correcting the dog. In this second week, the aim is to teach the dog that he will be rewarded for paying attention, and that he will always receive a reward even if the reward is not in sight.

WEEK THREE
The third week of Attention training should find the dog happily paying attention, even if there is no visible reward. At this point, the food reward is extended into three phases: one-third out of the hand (visible), one-third out of the hand (out of sight), and one-third left in the pocket to be given as reward after the dog has paid attention once you have shown him that both hands are empty of food. As in week two, if the dog keeps paying attention after you have shown him that your hands are empty, praise him, and reward him by producing food out of your pocket. If the dog looks away, correct him, then praise and reward him once you have got his attention back.

SUMMARY
In the three-week period, you have started off by teaching the dog to pay attention for short periods while being visually offered food, and in the last two weeks you have removed the visual food aid and kept his attention with voice praise. By the end of this three-week period, you should be able to keep the dog's attention while you take a couple of steps to the left or right, without having to tempt the dog with visual food rewards. The dog should be confident that he will always be rewarded if he keeps paying attention.

AVOIDING MISTAKES
It is important to teach the dog the three phases of reward training in this basic Attention step, because in all the Attention and Heelwork steps, we will use these same three phases. The dog must be taught to happily and willingly pay attention, with or without the visual aid of his reward. How many times have you seen a dog giving excellent Attention and doing beautiful Heelwork, as long as his toy or food is in sight only to see the whole thing fall to pieces the moment the visual aid is removed? This is caused by the handler making the mistake of *always* having the reward in sight, thereby making the reward the command or signal to work. In other words, to the dog's way of thinking, he only has to pay attention if his reward is in sight.

We often compound this first mistake by assuming that if the dog can do lovely Heelwork with the reward in sight, he should also understand – without being taught – that he can do it without the visual aid. If the dog fails to understand, he is punished. This results in the dog happily working for a visual reward but resenting all work without the visual aid, which is the exact opposite of what is intended – and all because we did not understand the correct use of motivation and rewards.

To establish the lessons taught to the dog in the first three weeks, you will need to vary both the number of food rewards given and the length of time between each piece of food.

Never forget that the food reward is a training aid and must not become the dog's only motivation to work. The reward is used to emphasise verbal praise, not to replace it.

In this same period, the dog has learnt to recognise the tone of voice when used as praise and for giving a command. Just as during puppy training, only introduce the command once the dog is already doing what you want him to do. In this instance, the Watch command is only given when the dog is already paying attention. All that we require of the dog in this period is that he pays attention while you move around the training area.

ATTENTION IN THE SIT

In puppy training, the pup was taught to sit by holding food above his head, rewarded for sitting, and then given the command once he had sat. This same technique can be used when training an older dog, and once the dog has been taught to sit, the next step of Attention training can be taught.

Attention in the Sit

Wait until your dog is paying attention. Give the Sit command, while holding the food reward above the dog's head. Gradually extend the time the dog sits before giving the reward, and extend the distance until you can stand anywhere within the length of the lead.

Attention at Heel

Stand in front of your dog, holding the food in your left hand. Give the command "Sit", and then twizzle into the Heel position.

Start off by repeating the first step of Attention training, and once the dog is paying attention give the Sit command while holding food above his head. Praise the dog for sitting, then release him and give him the food reward. Gradually increase the length of time between giving the Sit and the Release command until the dog can, if required, sit for a full minute. Remember to continually talk to the dog. Keep him interested by giving him several pieces of food during the Sit exercise, but make sure to vary the amount given each time.

Take a step or two to the left or right, gradually working up to the point where you can walk anywhere within the length of your lead, while the dog sits happily paying attention. Remember the three phases of food reward: visual in hand, out of sight in hand, and in the pocket, and, as with each new step of all exercises, take the dog through all three phases. By now you should be able to hold the dog's attention while walking to and fro, holding the end of a loose lead, without the visual aid of food or toy.

ATTENTION AT HEEL

A natural extension to Attention in the Sit is Attention at Heel, and, once again, you can teach the dog an extremely important exercise without demanding anything new from the dog.

Command the dog to Sit, as in the previous step, then, with food held above his head in the left hand, twizzle slowly to the left until you are in the Heel position. (The term 'twizzle', which is used repeatedly in this book, describes a movement used during training when the handler positions himself in the Heelwork position by turning to the left and stepping back, rather than insisting that the dog moves into the Heelwork position.) Because you know what you want to do (and the dog does not), it is far easier to position yourself next to the dog, thereby making sure that the dog is sitting perfectly straight at Heel, rather than trying to teach the dog to position himself next to you. All the dog has to do is co-operate, and to sit still as he has already been taught to do in the previous step. Once you are in the Heel position, you can introduce the (new) command "Heel", then praise, release and reward him.

As in all new steps, you must not forget to go through the three phases of food reward in order to establish the voice praise as more important than the food reward.

MAKING PROGRESS

You have now taught your dog to pay attention while moving (step 1), to pay attention in the Sit (step 2), and to pay attention at Heel (step 3). By careful choice of a training area with no distractions, the use of abundant rewards and praise, and restricting the duration of the training sessions to a couple of minutes, you should now have a happy, willing, attentive dog that is ready to learn other exercises.

However, before proceeding further, take a close look at your progress to date. You must be confident that the dog has thoroughly understood the lessons taught, and you must fully appreciate the importance of the three phases of reward. Special attention should be given to the dog's confidence and attitude, as any hesitation or apathy will be magnified in later training. If you are not completely satisfied with your progress, another week or two invested in building the dog's confidence will be time well spent.

Attention training is the foundation of all further training and is the most important exercise that the dog must learn. Therefore we should only proceed once the dog is ready to do so.

Chapter Four

DEPORTMENT AND FOOTWORK

GENERAL DEPORTMENT

In the last thirty years or so, Obedience has developed into a highly competitive sport, far removed from its origins in basic pet dog training. I realised early on in my career that training a dog to perform to perfection was only possible if the handler was as highly-schooled as the dog, with each movement being carefully taught and rehearsed.

Competition Obedience is teamwork, with both dog and handler performing as a team in complete harmony with each other. Charlie Wyant was the first trainer to pass on to me the importance of good deportment, both in training and in formal competition. Charlie's footwork is probably the most well-known basic footwork technique used in British Obedience. Using Charlie's basic methods, instructors like myself have taken deportment much further than just footwork. I believe that body language, from head to toe, should be developed in such a way that the dog, taking its clues from the handler, will, from the moment it enters the ring, receive and understand continuous signals from the handler. This will allow the dog to perform as one with his partner, seemingly without extra commands, although, in fact, the handler's deportment is constantly commanding the dog.

If you are not aware of the signals that you are transmitting to the dog, you will, as often as not, send the wrong signal thereby causing confusion. You have taught the dog to pay attention and to concentrate on every move that you make, so if you do not learn to control your body language, you will be unaware that you are the cause of your dog's mistakes. Whether competing in the ring or working in general training sessions, I hold the principle that if my dog is paying attention, and therefore following my every lead, then all mistakes made must be my fault. The only mistake the dog can make is lack of attention.

Later on, I will describe how I have developed my deportment, and I will use my method as an example. However, it would be wrong to rely on copying the way I (or any other instructor) walk and move. Deportment is a very personal thing and is determined by many different factors: your body shape, your fitness, the size and type of dog you are working, and many other variations. I could never attempt to walk like Charlie Wyant or for that matter like my wife, Ria. We are all built differently and train different types of dogs, but we do approach the subject of deportment in the same way because we all realise the

Good deportment and footwork are the key to competing successfully in Obedience. Your dog reads your body language and will pick up clues – which may be correct or incorrect – from the way you are moving.

importance of body language and its influence on our dogs. In my beginners class I spend as much time teaching the principles of good deportment as I do training the dogs. Later, when I am teaching Attention training, I try to impress on the (human) pupil that individual deportment should be developed before starting to teach the formal exercises. I have lost count of the number of times that I have seen beginner (and sometimes advanced) handlers saying one thing with their voice while countermanding the verbal command with conflicting body language. Many trainers believe that body language and deportment only applies to the Heelwork exercise, but, in fact, it is equally important in all the exercises. The principle of good deportment becomes amplified in Heelwork because the exercise is of longer duration than all the other Obedience exercises, with the exception of the Stays.

There are most probably some trainers who have so much natural ability that they do not have to consciously teach themselves good deportment – they have been born with this gift. I was not so lucky. Most of us mere mortals have to constantly struggle to develop a style of deportment that is complementary to, and not in conflict with, our dogs, and which is acceptable within the rules and regulations of Obedience competitions. We should also constantly bear in mind that what is acceptable within the confines of the Obedience ring should not restrict development in training. In the British Tests A, B and C, competitors cannot speak to their dogs, but they do so constantly in training. The same principle can be carried further in all teaching, as long as you are aware of how you communicate with your dog. One example of this is the handler who maintains eye contact throughout training, but stares ahead during Heelwork in competition, and then wonders why the dog performs so differently, usually accusing the dog of being ring-wise.

I believe that the dog only reacts differently because the handler is reacting differently. All these subtle differences can be minimised if deportment is so highly developed and practised that it becomes a habit. A habit is something we do subconsciously, and if we have made a habit of correct deportment we will be able to transmit the same signals to the dog under the stress of competition, as we do in training. All competitors are nervous and stressed in the ring (at least those of us that are human!), but if good deportment is a habit, we will still perform correctly. The first step in developing good deportment is realising its importance. Deportment is not just teaching yourself good footwork; it encompasses complete body movement, including facial expression, eye contact, and body posture. It is a combination of being aware of how we move naturally and schooled body movements, and these should never be inhibiting for dog or handler.

The description of deportment that follows describes how I have taught myself to move. It is the principles that are important. The actual methods are personal to me, and should, at best, be adapted to yourself rather than being imitated.

FOOTWORK

I always teach Charlie Wyant's method of footwork to beginners (the actual steps can be found in Chapter Six). It is the principle of footwork that is important – not just the way we turn – but every step we take. The length of step and how many steps taken per minute will be determined by your size in combination with the size and type of dog you are working. It would be wrong to expect someone who is 5ft tall to take the same sized step, and work at the same pace, while working a Miniature Poodle as she would if she was working a German Shepherd Dog. Nor could we expect someone who is 6ft tall to step in the same way as somebody a foot shorter, even if they worked the same dog.

I have to shorten my pace to work Woolie, my current Test C dog, whereas with Wimp, my previous Test C dog, I could take longer, and (for me) easier steps, while not reducing his style of work. Both dogs were Collies and of similar weight and height, although built quite differently. With Woolie, I need to pace at one particular tempo if I want him to be collected. If I fail to get it right, the dog works on his front end, alters his head position, and will often amble. Years ago, I would have blamed the dog for not trying hard enough.

Obviously, you cannot determine stride and pace until you start Heelwork with your dog, but you can teach yourself to walk fluently and smoothly, and then adapt your pace, if necessary, when working the dog. Start by walking a complete C without a dog, and then train yourself to walk weaves and circles, including changes of pace. Starting and halting correctly should also be perfected. In fact, the Halt highlights the importance of good footwork.

Let us take as an example someone who walks 120 steps per minute. That means two steps per second, or that each foot touches the ground once each second. When halting, I stop on the right foot and close up on the left. Logically speaking, the left leg only takes half a step to close up to the right, and therefore should only take half the time, as it is only travelling half the distance. However, this is not the case. When teaching the Halt, without the dog, I count out one, two, one, two, as I walk. As I close the left leg up to the right leg to halt, the beat stays the same. This means that the left leg is travelling only half the distance at the same beat, and so it must slow down. When doing this with a dog, the dog will realise that the Sit is coming (once he has been taught) by reading my body language. I use this example only to demonstrate that the dog who is paying attention will pick up on the most subtle body signals. In actual fact, I take half-steps – left leg up to right – in all turns as well as to the Halt, so it is a combination of body signals that tells the dog what is happening, not just the change of pace.

Correct footwork enables the handler to be balanced and to perfect his general deportment; it does not tell the dog which way to turn. After all the dog is looking up, and not watching the feet. Too many people learn correct footwork and ignore the rest of deportment, and would rather blame the dog for incorrect work.

BODY POSTURE

Posture is also determined by build. A tall person working a small dog will tend to bend more than a small person working a Great Dane. Bending (in training) as such is not wrong, so long as you realise that it could become a signal to the dog. If you are teaching the Halt, using the footwork (explained later), and you bend over to watch the dog into the Sit every time that you halt, the dog will most probably see the bending of the body as the command to Sit, instead of the change of pace, because the bend is far more imposing and blatant than the subtle change in pace. Sometimes we cannot prevent these potential bad habits, but so long as we are aware that they must not be constant, we can avoid unintentional signals becoming *the* body signal. Every time that you work your dog, he will start to recognise body signals which tell him what to do. It is essential to ensure that the *only* signals that are constant are the ones that you will use in the ring, and that are acceptable within the rules for competition.

I imagine that my spinal column is the source of all my body movements, and it therefore determines my deportment. My spine is the centre of a circle, with my shoulders as the outside of the circle. I imagine that my vertebrae are fixed and cannot turn independently of each other. In this way, I can prevent myself from twisting my body when doing turns. My spine can rotate on its own axis, but not circle, which prevents me from bending forward or sideways. This does not mean that I never bend over my dog, it just means that when I do so, I am aware that I am doing so. Obviously, you do not want to walk so stiffly and unnaturally that you become robot-like. It is a matter of finding the balance between smooth fluent movement and correct deportment, while being aware that the dog is watching your every move.

In right and about-turn, I imagine that my left shoulder, which is the outside of the circle, must complete either a quarter or half-turn without speeding up or slowing down, and without my body twisting to the right. If I twist my body going into a turn, I will cause the dog to speed up in an attempt to maintain his position. This means the dog will then have to slow down as I straighten up, coming out of the turn. I want my dog to maintain the same tempo in the turns as in a straight line, and I have found that imagining my spine as the centre of the circle is the most effective way of achieving this aim.

HEAD POSITION AND EYE CONTACT
Almost all training is taught to the dog while we are looking at him. Initially, it is almost impossible not to look at the dog. Eye contact is good and necessary in training, and it is an important part of your relationship with your dog. However, we should also teach the dog to work just as well without eye contact.

This is necessary to enable the handler to walk correctly in the ring, which is impossible if you are turning to the right while looking to the left (at the dog). I prefer to position my head so that, with my eyes straight, I am looking at the ground about two to three yards ahead of me. Without moving my head, I can then lift my eyes to see where I am going, or look down at my dog out of the corner of my eye. When turning, I look to the ground two or three yards ahead, just as in the straight line. While working, my eyes alternate between looking ahead and looking at the dog, and in this way the dog realises that he can work without eye contact, and will therefore maintain his position while I look ahead. The occasional glance at the dog during competition can be done without any head movement, and so should not be seen as an extra command.

The handler's body language and deportment is constantly sending signals to the dog. We must therefore train ourselves to walk and move in a way that is both complementary to the dog and acceptable within the rules of competition. The principle that if the dog is paying attention, all other faults must stem from the handler, should prevent us from blaming the dog for our mistakes. If we fail to realise the importance of deportment in Obedience training, this will mean that we are under-estimating a significant aspect of training dogs.

LEAD TECHNIQUE

I was once told that the word 'lead' is an abbreviation of the word 'leader', and this was how the lead should be used, as a leader or guide, and not as a weapon or form of restraint. I prefer to use a simple leather or rope lead and a leather collar when training. I also believe that the type of training equipment used is of less importance than *how* it is used. I vary the way I hold the lead, depending on the type of dog and the stage of training. I explain to my pupils the various ways of how the lead can be held, and thereafter they are allowed to hold the lead in the way they find most comfortable.

The lead should be seen as an extension of the arm, through which you have physical contact with your dog. Over-use of the lead, either by harshness or by constantly being too tight, can cause untold damage to a dog's confidence. The lead should be short enough so that you can tighten the lead without exaggerated arm movements, while at the same time making sure it is not so short that it is constantly tugging at the dog.

LEAD IN THE LEFT HAND
With the lead held in the left hand, you can walk while swinging the right arm. I always hold my lead in the left hand in competition, and when training an experienced dog. The right hand can then swing naturally which helps maintain balance, and it can also be used to close the dog up in the right turns. As you make a turn, the right hand can swing across the body to grasp and draw the lead to the right, to keep the dog in position. This method is suitable for right and about-turns, but it will not work for the left turns and Halts.

LEAD IN THE RIGHT HAND
If the lead is held in the right hand, at about chest height, the left hand can slide down the lead and be used as a funnel to trap the lead to the body in the turns. This left hand movement can then be used as a signal when working the dog off lead. I prefer to use this method only once the dog is fairly well-advanced in training. The lead must be held in this way when first teaching the basics of the left turns.

When first teaching the basic Heelwork steps to beginner handlers, I teach them to hold the lead in the right hand, with the right arm just hanging naturally at the side. In this way, the lead will not be misused and the dog will be able to find his balance during Heelwork. In the turns, the lead can be drawn to the right to tighten the dog up, with the same simple movement being used if the dog drifts off from the left leg.

The advantage of using the lead in this way is that it is very simple, and does not involve difficult techniques. I find that beginner handlers have enough to think about without the additional worry of an intricate lead technique. I see this as an acceptable compromise, and once the handlers feel comfortable with footwork, timing and such like, they can always improve the lead technique to polish up their performance.

LEAD TIMING
The timing of commands and footwork is of paramount importance when learning to do turns, and in this situation, the lead timing should coincide with the voice command. For example, in the right turn the dog's name is given as the left foot is forward (at which time

the right hand reaches across to draw the lead across the body), then, as the right foot comes forward, the command for the right turn is given, (as the lead is drawn to the right to close the dog up). The left foot then tees to the right (the right hand on the lead will hold the dog in position), and then the right foot steps out of the turn, and as the left leg comes forward, the right hand is removed from the lead.

If the lead is held in the right hand, the left hand will guide the dog by sliding down the lead, but the timing will remain the same. In all turns, both to left and right, the timing will be the same: taking the slack up as the left foot is forward and holding the dog in position until the first step has been taken out of the turn, at which time the pressure is released.

I always use the lead to play tug-of-war with my dogs, and I finish off every training session with this game. The lead is the ideal toy as it is the only toy that is allowed in the ring.

PRINCIPLES OF FOOTWORK

Good deportment is a combination of correct footwork and balance. However, footwork is the means to a goal and not a goal in itself. It would be wrong to have perfect mathematical footwork if the rest of your body signals are not correctly co-ordinated. Footwork is one of the aids that may be used in the ring without penalty, and by making a turn each time in the same way the dog will learn to take his clues from our body language seemingly without a command.

Once the footwork has been learnt, it should be practised without the dog until it becomes a habit that can be performed without conscious thought. This will result in the handler developing a rhythm that will enhance both the handler and the dog's performance. I teach Charlie Wyant's basic steps to all my beginner handlers and once the footwork becomes routine, the technique can, if needed, be slightly adapted to ensure balance at all times. It would be wrong to expect a plump, middle-aged person to be as agile as a young slim teenager. It is the principle of footwork that is important: starting off, halting and making each turn in the same way, with the same timing each time.

The timing of footwork, commands and aids should be uniform, and I use a method which I call the 'One, Two, Three timing':

One is the dog's name.
Two is the command.
Three is the movement.

When starting off in Heelwork, I would call the dog's name (One), give the command "Heel" (Two), and then step off with the left leg (Three). In a right turn, I would call the dog's name as the left foot is forward (One), give the command as the right foot is forward (Two), and then tee to the right with the left foot (Three). The timing remains the same for all turns, and also for the Halt. In this way the timing, together with the footwork and the aids will help the dog to understand what is required.

The left leg is the leading leg in Heelwork and will signal the dog when to start, when to

LEAD TECHNIQUE

The lead is held in the left hand, so the right hand can be used to draw the dog in.

The lead is held in the right hand, so the left hand can be used as a funnel to guide the dog into position.

The lead is held in the right hand, and is drawn to the right in order to close the dog in.

turn, in which direction to turn, and when to halt. When starting off, the left leg takes the first step, and when halting, the last step, (stop on the right and close up with the left). All turns are taught in the same way, by stopping on the right and teeing to the left or right.

RIGHT TURN

As the left leg is forward, the dog's name is given. As the right foot comes forward, the command "Heel" is given, and the left foot is placed across the toe of the right foot to turn to the right. The right foot then leads out of the turn.

ABOUT-TURN

The about-turn is, in fact, a double right turn, with the timing and command being the same as when making a right turn. Stop on the right foot and tee with the left, as in the right turn. Then reverse the right foot 180 degrees, so that the heel of the right foot is placed by the instep of the left. Step out of the turn on the left foot.

LEFT TURN

Stop on the right foot and tee with the left, as in the right turn, only this time the left foot is pointing to the left. Step out of the turn on the right foot. It is possible to step out of the turn on the left foot by placing the right foot next to the left after making the tee, and then transferring the weight to the right foot before stepping out on the left. This gives larger dogs the time to tuck in, although some judges may decide that the handler has stopped in the turn. This does not mean that it cannot be included as a training aid.

In training, it will be necessary to step back in the left turn to teach the dog to tuck in. To do this, stop on the right and tee with the left, and then turn 90 degrees to the left and step back with the right, before stepping out of the turn on the right. The step back can also be done with the left leg by placing the right foot next to the left after teeing, then transferring the weight to the right before stepping back with the left. This prevents the dog from overturning as the left leg restricts the dog's movement.

LEFT ABOUT-TURN

The left about-turn is an extension of the left turn. Stop on the right and tee with the left, then place the toe of the right foot into the instep of the left. Turn 90 degrees with the left foot and then step out on the right foot. In training, it is also possible to adapt the left about-turn. Teach the dog to tuck in by stopping on the right and making a tee with the left. Then place the right foot next to the left, and turn the left foot 90 degrees to the left so that the heel of the left foot is in the instep of the right foot. The right foot can then be placed next to the left, and a step back can be taken with the left foot to tuck the dog in. Alternatively, instead of placing the right foot next to the left, just step out of the turn on the right foot. This is another method for left about-turns.

SUMMARY

The secret of learning these turns is correct transference of weight from one foot to the other to keep in balance. However, for the footwork to be of any use whatsoever, it must be practised without a dog until it becomes second nature. To attempt to train a dog before being able to complete these turns without thinking about them, would lead to confusion and frustration for both dog and handler.

Once both handler and dog are experienced and working well as a team, a style of work will develop that will necessitate adaption of the basic footwork techniques. However, I always insist that all my pupils start off by learning the basic steps which are then used as a foundation for evolving their own personal style.

Chapter Five

HEELWORK I: GETTING STARTED

Before starting on Heelwork, it is worthwhile to recap progress to date. You have taught your dog to pay attention while you move about the training area, you have progressed to Attention in the Sit and continued to teach Attention while the dog is sitting at Heel. Up until now, the priority has been Attention. However, we have also taught the dog the Watch, Sit and Heel position commands. By making use of the lessons your dog has learned so far, you are ready to teach basic Heelwork. Just as in the previous lessons, do not forget the three phases of reward, and make sure you use them continuously throughout the training.

STEP ONE: THE FIRST STEPS OF HEELWORK
Start off with the dog paying attention as in Step One of Attention training. The lead should be in your right hand and the food (toy) reward in the left. Guide the dog towards you by backing away from him. At the moment that the dog is standing in the Present, twizzle back to the left and position yourself in the Heelwork position. Your left hand, with the food in it, has moved to your left leg just above the dog's head and approximately level with the seam of your trousers. All the dog has had to do is follow your left hand while moving forward in a straight line. You have turned to the dog, not the other way round.

Do not attempt to do any Heelwork, just praise the dog for co-operating and give him the Heelwork command as he comes into the Heelwork position. This movement is more difficult than it sounds, but it is only difficult for the handler, the dog just has to co-operate. Remember to give the Heelwork command only when the dog is in the correct position. Repeat this step several times per training session until you can see that the dog understands that he will be rewarded for being in the Heel position. It is important that you do not neglect the other basic Attention steps. This step is an addition to the basic Attention training steps, it is not a replacement.

STEP TWO: LEFT CIRCLE
You can now start to introduce one or two steps of Heelwork before releasing and rewarding your dog. Start off with just one step, and increase one or two steps at a time until you can complete a left-hand circle of about 30 to 40 steps. Never forget to alternate how many steps

Learning the left-hand circle.

of Heelwork you do. One time do ten steps, the next time three, then seven, and so on, so that the dog never knows when he is going to be rewarded. You must always remember to introduce the three phases of reward once the dog is confident, so that he does not get the chance to misunderstand and presume that he only has to work if the reward is in sight.

When you are doing the left-hand circle, the lead will be in the right hand which will hang naturally by your right-hand side. If the dog drifts off a little to the left, you can gently tug him in with the lead to the right, horizontal to the ground. If the dog is leaning away to the left, the lead should be brought up to chest level and, once again, with gentle diagonal tugs, the dog can be brought back into position. Remember at all times to praise and encourage the dog with your voice and body movements, or the food reward will become too important. Always remember that the food (toy) is a training aid only, and that you should be the main source of motivation.

If you find that the dog is happy when the reward is in sight (phase 1), but is less so if the reward is out of sight (phases 2 & 3), then you have made two possible mistakes. You may have relied too much on the food and failed to praise the dog verbally, or you have not balanced out the three phases of reward. In both cases, the solution is to go back to Step One of Attention training and start again. Throughout training you must make a habit of observing the dog's attitude while going from step to step. With correct training, there should be no change in attitude whatsoever.

The left-hand circle is the easiest way of introducing a dog to Heelwork and will teach him his position on the move. The handler is working to the dog while in the left-hand circle, and it is therefore easier to maintain eye contact, which initially is something we want to do. However, once the dog is working with confidence we should start to break eye contact and gradually start to look a yard or two ahead while praising the dog.

A common fault is to constantly maintain eye contact in training, resulting in the dog coming forward in competition in an attempt to keep eye contact. So the dog must be weaned off this misunderstanding gradually. This does not mean that you must never look at your dog. It just means that the dog should be taught that he must watch us while maintaining his Heel position, even when we are not watching him. We start this off in the left-hand circle and reinforce it in the right-hand circle.

STEP THREE: RIGHT CIRCLE

This circle is more difficult for the handler than for the dog, because in the right-hand circle the dog can still watch you, but you have more problem in seeing him. The handler must imagine the circle that he must walk, and should look at this imaginary circle with the eyes looking down about two to three yards ahead. The techniques for reward and lead use are the same as in the left-hand circle. The major difference is that the dog is on the outside. Therefore you are working away from him, and you have broken eye contact.

The previous steps have taught the dog to pay attention and to maintain a Heel position, and we are helping the dog with the same technique as in the left-hand circle, so this step should be straightforward for the dog. However, many handlers do have a problem in the right circle, mainly because they do not have the confidence to work the dog without looking at him. This step teaches the dog to read the handler's body, and if you are walking to the right while (wrongly) looking to the left, you will be defeating the object of the lesson.

As in the left circle, start off with only one or two steps and gradually build up to a thirty or forty-step right circle, which the dog should do as happily and correctly as the left-hand circle, but with the major difference that there is no direct eye contact. In the left-hand circle, you are always working towards the dog and you are always in eye contact with him. In the right circle, you will break this potentially bad habit. At this stage it is perhaps worth mentioning the handler's head position. I prefer to look at the ground about two to three

Learning the right-hand circle.

yards ahead. In this way, I can lift my eyes to look ahead to where I am going, without moving my head. Or I can look at the dog out of the corner of my eye, once again without moving my head. Trial and error will decide your ideal head position, which will be influenced by the size of your dog.

STEP FOUR: FIGURE-OF-EIGHT

Teaching the figure-of-eight is a matter of combining the two previous steps and should, therefore, cause little or no problem. Once again, it is important that the handler performs his or her part of the work correctly. I prefer to imagine the invisible 'eight' marked out before me, and to look at the ground two or three yards ahead. In this way, when the dog is on the inside we can see each other quite easily, and when the dog is on the outside, he can watch me while I am looking away from him.

An additional bonus is that when I am crossing over from the left circle to the right, or vice versa, I will use these few steps to purposely look down and make eye contact with the dog. In this way you are, within the forty or so steps of the figure of eight, making eye contact (on the straight), having the dog in view (in the left circle), and looking away from him (in the right circle), thereby combining all the previous steps. The dog is also learning

Figure-of-eight, with the dog working on the inside.

Figure-of-eight, with the dog working on the outside.

to read your body movements, which are constantly changing to the left, right, and straight. However, this will only work if you have taught yourself to position your body and work a figure-of-eight properly. The reward and lead techniques remain the same as in the previous steps.

STEP FIVE: THE WEAVE

I believe that the weave is the most important of all the basic Heelwork steps, in that it teaches the dog to read your body movements and combines all the previous Heelwork steps in one exercise. However it is only useful as a teaching exercise if we fully understand what we are teaching at this stage. If done properly, the dog will learn to read and understand the subtle body language which tells him which direction we are going to turn and will teach him to hold his position wherever we walk. We can also introduce the commands for left and right turns which will simplify the teaching of turns later on.

Start off by placing seven or eight small cones or poles five steps apart in a straight line. Place another cone at the end of the row about ten yards away. Before you can teach the dog to work a weave, you must learn to weave competently and naturally yourself. So while holding the left hand in the Heelwork position, just walk up the line of cones while weaving in and out in a natural way. Keep your eyes on the end cone and do not attempt to look down at the ground. By doing this without the dog, you will learn to balance yourself and to turn your body in a natural way. Remember to keep your eyes on the last cone in the row each time you do the weave. This will make your body turn naturally. Once *you* feel comfortable, you can start to teach your dog.

To avoid confusion and mistakes, you must bear in mind that you are teaching the dog to read your body movements. Therefore it is essential that you carry out your part of the exercise correctly, and move the same way with the dog as without. To do this, bring the dog into the Heelwork position, place your left hand in the Heelwork position and hold the lead in the right hand, making sure that the lead is loose so that it will not influence the dog. Start to weave through the cones, ignoring the dog if he bumps your leg while on the inside or drifts off while on the outside. The dog should only be corrected for not paying attention. At this stage we should just ignore technical imperfections. If you have taught the previous lessons correctly, you will find that within two or three attempts the dog has started to read your body language.

I always get a kick out of watching the surprise on a pupil's face when their dog successfully completes a seemingly difficult exercise within a minute or two of first attempting it. Once again, all you have done is combined the lessons learned in the previous steps, reinforcing the lesson that the dog must learn to read body signals. If you had not taught the dog to do the right-hand circle, and had not been aware of the danger of constantly maintaining eye contact, the weave would have been much more difficult to teach. No one can walk a weave while watching a dog, i.e. walking to the right while looking to the left.

Once the dog is maintaining the Heel position in the weave, you can tighten him up by using the lead tugs, either horizontally or diagonally, as in the previous steps, while at the same time introducing the commands for left turns and right turns. I do this one at a time,

*The weave:
This teaches
the dog to read
your body
language while
you curve to
the left, with
the dog on the
inside.*

*The weave:
This teaches
the dog to read
your body
language while
you curve to
the right, with
the dog on the
outside.*

starting with the right turn. As I weave with the cones on my right and the dog on the outside of the curve, I give him the command for the right turn because I am turning slightly to the right and the dog must turn with me. So on alternate cones, I can introduce the command for right turn. Once this has been taught, I will start to give the left turn command when the cone is on my left. I will be curving slightly to the left into the dog, and will introduce, on alternate cones, the left turn command. Later on, as the dog becomes confident and experienced, I will combine both commands and will weave through the cones saying: "Close (left), good boy"; "Heel (right), good boy" and so on. In this way, the verbal command combined with the body language will make the teaching of the turns far easier.

As previously stated, I believe that the weave is the most important of the basic Heelwork exercises. It is a pity that so many trainers treat it as an advanced exercise and therefore do not teach it until the dog is qualified for the higher classes.

SUMMARY

If we review this phase of training, we can see that we have taught the dog the left circle, right circle, figure-of-eight, and the weave. All these exercises encourage the dog to do smooth, flowing Heelwork. They establish the dog's Heel position and teach him to read body language. The dog has been taught to watch the handler even if the handler is not watching him, and the lead technique for turns has been introduced. At the end of this phase of training the dog should be happy and confident, and you can start the next stage of training, which includes starting from the Halt, the basic turns, and the Halt. All of which we have intentionally avoided until the dog is confident and knows how to maintain his Heel position.

Chapter Six

HEELWORK II: NOVICE WORK

Before starting on the next phase of Heelwork training, we should take a good look at the progress we have made to date. Attention training, combined with the first phase of Heelwork, should have resulted in a happy, confident dog who knows his Heelwork position and can maintain this position as you walk, while curving to the left or right. The dog is happy to read your body language for clues instead of listening purely to voice commands. His rewards (either food or toys) have been phased so that his attitude is unchanged whether the reward is in sight or not. The dog has been taught to maintain his position in left and right circles, and in the figure-of-eight and the weave. All these steps have been used to develop happy fluent Heelwork, so if – and only if – you are happy with the progress made, you can now start on the next phase of Heelwork.

STARTING FROM THE HALT

It should by now be obvious that we always try to introduce one new lesson at a time to the dog. In this step, the aim is to teach the dog to start Heelwork from the Halt. The dog knows his Heelwork position while sitting at Heel from Step Three of Attention training, and he knows his position on the move from basic Heelwork training. The task is now to combine these basic steps and teach the dog to heel starting from the Halt.

Tell the dog to sit and twizzle into the Heelwork position. The lead should be just loose enough to allow the dog to move off on command, without lead influence. While remembering to incorporate the 1,2,3 timing, give the dog the Heel command and step off with the left foot. The moment that the dog moves, praise him for moving and then release and reward him. Do not attempt to actually do any Heelwork. One, or at most two steps (for large dogs) is all that you should do. The dog should have little problem in understanding because you are only combining previously-taught steps in a different situation. If the dog does not move off with the left leg, a slight tug on the lead combined with lots of praise will get him moving. It is important that you take no more than one or two steps at this stage because you only want to teach the dog to move with the left leg. If you were to carry on heeling (which the dog can already do), you would distract from the new step being taught.

Few, if any, dogs have problems understanding this new step, and this is often mistakenly

The dog should be in the Heel position, with the lead loose enough so that the dog can move off, on command, without lead influence.

Remember to incorporate the 1,2,3 timing, give the Heel command, and step off on the left foot.

The Halt: teaching the dog to sit, applying all the aids.

interpreted by the handler as a reason not to bother teaching this step as a separate exercise. By limiting the amount of steps to one or two, you will not allow hesitation to creep into your training, but will once again give the dog something simple to do, and by doing so, will build confidence.

The layout of most show rings means that a dog rarely has to Heel for more than fifteen or twenty steps in any one direction before either turning or halting. Therefore, all we have to do is teach the dog to Heel in a straight line for up to twenty steps. By building up from the one or two steps, starting from the Halt, you can gradually increase the amount of Heelwork steps taken until, at the end of this phase of training, the dog will happily move off into Heelwork from the Halt, expecting at any moment to be praised and released.

The last thing that you want is for the dog to assume that he will be heeling for the next five minutes. To maintain his attitude and motivation, the dog should expect Heelwork to be short and exciting. Twenty steps of Heelwork will only take about ten seconds, which is well within the dog's concentration span. Throughout this whole phase of training, do not take more than twenty steps without releasing the dog. The amount of steps taken should be constantly varied, with the dog never knowing when he will be released. Twenty steps will be more than enough to start incorporating turns, so if you condition yourself not to take more than twenty steps, you will remove the risk of the dog becoming bored by doing endless Heelwork.

HALT AS STATIC

Once again, you do not have to do a complete Heelwork round to incorporate a Halt. The previous steps of Attention training and basic Heelwork have taught the dog to maintain his position, and this combined with your own correct deportment will simplify the teaching of the Halt. You certainly do not want to start correcting the dog for a crooked Sit, so you must bear in mind the principle that if the dog is paying attention, all other mistakes that he makes are your fault.

To teach the Halt, place the dog in the Sit and twizzle into the Heelwork position. Tell the dog to sit, and, leading with the right leg, take one step forward. Step back with the left leg, give the dog the Heel command and close the left leg up to the right. As the dog closes up, apply the aids: bring the right hand which is holding the lead across the body and tighten the lead, and at the same time use the middle finger of the left hand to exert gentle pressure on the dog's right flank to ensure a straight Sit. The lead in the right hand should be vertical and above the dog's head, and the left hand should never push down on the dog's spine. Although this will entail some bending, try to keep your body as straight as possible by bending the knees rather than leaning forward over the dog.

The dog will, in fact, go from one Sit straight into another, and if you have got your deportment right and applied the aids with the correct timing, he will be sitting straight. However, if you find that this is not the case, you will have to think back and decide what went wrong. Nine times out of ten, the cause of the crooked Sit was a deportment fault or wrong application of the aids, both of which are handler faults. Most often, it is because you are bending over and looking at the dog. A straight Sit is a combination of attention, the dog knowing his position, and the handler – through good deportment – giving the dog a clear signal together with a verbal command. The only mistake that is the dog's fault is lack of attention. A crooked Sit by a dog paying attention means that the handler made a mistake. The solution lies with the handler's deportment and timing, and this must be corrected before you carry on teaching the Halt.

HALT ON THE MOVE

Presuming that progress has been made and the dog has been taught to sit straight, you can continue and incorporate a few steps of Heelwork before halting. By using the same verbal command and deportment as in the static step, teach the dog to sit as you halt, always remembering to apply the aids.

When you taught yourself deportment, you learned to stop on the right foot and close up with the left, while keeping your body straight and looking at the ground about two or three yards ahead, so obviously you must do the same now. In actual fact, if your basic work has been done correctly, you do not have to actually teach the dog anything that he does not already know. Once again, you are combining known steps in a new situation. Do not release the dog immediately that he is in the Sit, but let him sit for four or five seconds while you praise him. Releasing too quickly can cause slow Sits because, to the dog's way of thinking, the moment he sits he will be released, so why should he bother sitting?

Once the dog is sitting happily from Heelwork, you can introduce the Halt into your straight line Heelwork (never more than twenty steps), before releasing and rewarding the dog. The dog should now be able to start from the Sit at Heel, do up to twenty steps of Heelwork, and sit correctly as you halt. The number of steps taken from one Sit to the next must be constantly varied. It is important to bear in mind that the more Heelwork you do, the more the dog has to think about, thus the more you will distract him from thinking about the lesson being taught, which, in this instance, is sitting straight.

CLOSING UP ON THE MOVE

Before starting to teach the turns, it is worthwhile teaching the dog to close up while on the move. This exercise will also help the dog to understand his Heelwork position, and later on it can be used as the basis for several other tightening-up exercises.

Start heeling the dog and as the right leg comes up to the left, touch the ground with the toe of the right foot and then take a step to the right. With your weight transferred to the right leg, step back with the left leg and close the dog up by taking the lead back. Praise the dog for being in the correct position, then release and reward him. Tipping the ground with

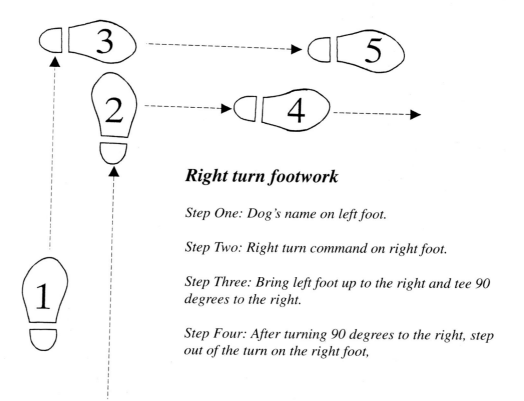

Right turn footwork

Step One: Dog's name on left foot.

Step Two: Right turn command on right foot.

Step Three: Bring left foot up to the right and tee 90 degrees to the right.

Step Four: After turning 90 degrees to the right, step out of the turn on the right foot,

the right foot next to the left before stepping to the right, will ensure that you stop forward movement before moving to the right. If you were just to step to the right you would move diagonally away from the dog, which is not what you want. Once the dog is confident in this movement, you can use it at any time when heeling to close the dog up into the correct Heel position.

RIGHT TURN

As with all steps taught to date, the right turn is taught as a separate exercise and only incorporated into the twenty steps of Heelwork once the dog understands the lesson. Before attempting to teach the dog, you will already have decided how to do a right turn, and you will have developed and practised your deportment. The golden rule with deportment is that it should be practised until it becomes a habit. A habit is something that we do subconsciously, i.e. without having to think about it. If you are trying to teach a dog a new step while thinking about your own part of the exercise, you will have a problem because no person can think of two things simultaneously. You will end up ignoring the dog to concentrate on yourself, or concentrating on the dog and ignoring your deportment. The only way forward is to train yourself until your part of the exercise can be done without thinking, and only then go on to teaching the dog.

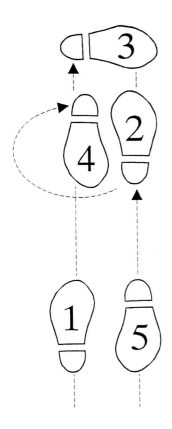

About-turn footwork.

Step One: Dog's name on left foot.

Step Two: Right turn command on right foot.

Step Three: Bring left foot up to the right and tee 90 degrees to the right.

Step Four: Turn right foot 180 degrees and place the heel by the instep of the left foot.

Step Five: Step out of the turn on the left foot.

RIGHT TURN AS STATIC

Place the dog in the Sit and twizzle to the Heel position. Take one step forward (two for a large dog). As in teaching Heelwork from the Halt, step back with the left leg, simultaneously give the dog the command for the right turn, and step forward, left leg up to right. This time, instead of sitting the dog, make a turn to the right and bring the dog round, using slight lead pressure to help him hold his position. The weave and the right circle have taught the dog to read your body and also taught him the right turn command; therefore make sure your deportment is correct to avoid confusion. After completing the turn, command the dog to sit. With a large dog, you may find it easier to take one step out of the turn, to give the dog room to straighten up, before the Sit. The praise for the turn should be given during the turn, not when the dog has completed the turn and is already sitting. At the risk of repeating myself, I must emphasise that if your deportment and timing are correct and the dog is paying attention, then nothing will go wrong – so make sure you have studied your deportment before attempting to teach the turn to the dog.

RIGHT TURN ON THE MOVE

Once the right turn as static has been taught, you can incorporate it into the twenty steps of straight line Heelwork – always bearing in mind that the fewer steps you do, the less the dog has to concentrate on. You must also make sure that your timing is correct. The dog's name is given on the left foot, and as the right foot comes forward, the right turn command is given. The left foot then makes a tee to the right, with the praise being given during the turn, not after the turn. Slight lead pressure to the right will ensure that the dog will keep his position. Do not carry on heeling after the turn, just take a step or two and then halt, praise, and release the dog before giving him his reward.

ABOUT-TURN AS STATIC

The about-turn is simply a double right turn, and should therefore be taught as such. Set the dog up as for the right turn, but this time instead of doing a 90-degree turn, complete a 180 degree turn, repeating the right turn command at 90 degrees. The most common mistake that is made in this turn – in fact, in teaching all turns – is to look down and back at the dog while attempting the turn. This, again, is a deportment fault. Your eyes should be looking at the ground a yard or two ahead. If you attempt to turn to the right while looking to the left, you will confuse the dog who will be reading your body language, and you will also lose your balance. Both these faults will result in an incorrect turn, with the dog losing position either by going wide or hanging back.

ABOUT-TURN ON THE MOVE

As with the right turn, introduce the about-turn into your twenty steps of Heelwork once the dog is happy and confident in the static. The command for the right turn and the about-turn is the same, although you may sometimes use the command a second time halfway through the about-turn. The lead technique is, as can be expected, the same. However, when using the lead, make sure that the pressure is only released once the dog has fully completed the turn.

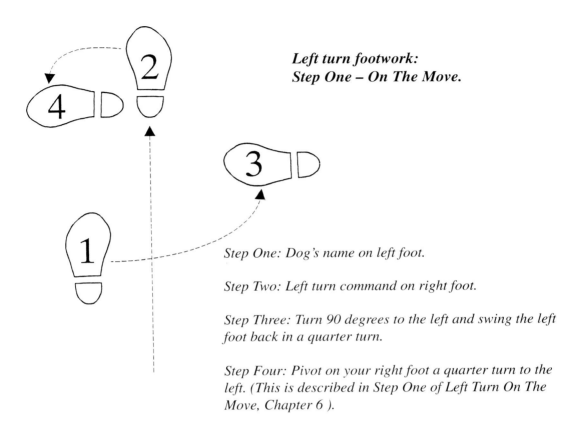

Left turn footwork:
Step One – On The Move.

Step One: Dog's name on left foot.

Step Two: Left turn command on right foot.

Step Three: Turn 90 degrees to the left and swing the left foot back in a quarter turn.

Step Four: Pivot on your right foot a quarter turn to the left. (This is described in Step One of Left Turn On The Move, Chapter 6).

LEFT TURN

This turn, more than any other, proves that good deportment and, more important, good timing is imperative. Some dogs will compensate for less than perfect timing in the right turns, covering up for sloppy handling and the handler's mistakes because the dog has room on the outside of the turn to maintain his position. However, in the left turn, and later in the left about-turn, the dog must read the body signal to turn left one step before the turn i.e. as the right leg is forward and the left leg back. The dog must have completed the tuck-in with his back end as the handler's left leg tees to the left. I have heard many instructors wrongly tell their pupils: "Stop on the right, tee with the left, and tuck the dog in". As you bring the left leg forward, the dog should already be turning; as the left foot is placed in the tee, the dog should already have completed his turn. This timing must be exact. If not, you will not be able to carry out the left turn correctly.

This is the reason we see so many dogs turning well in slow pace, where the dog can compensate to a certain degree, but failing to complete the same turn in normal or fast pace. The statics will teach the dog how to do the left turn, but without perfect timing he will

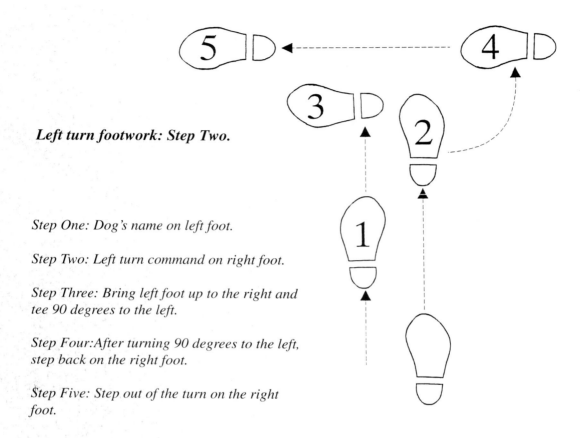

Left turn footwork: Step Two.

Step One: Dog's name on left foot.

Step Two: Left turn command on right foot.

Step Three: Bring left foot up to the right and tee 90 degrees to the left.

Step Four: After turning 90 degrees to the left, step back on the right foot.

Step Five: Step out of the turn on the right foot.

never be able to turn correctly on the move. So, once again, make sure your deportment and *timing* is correct before attempting to teach your dog.

LEFT TURN AS STATIC

Teaching the statics of the left turn is, in fact, the same as teaching the left-hand Finish. From the dog's point of view he will be making the same body movement, and so we can use the same command. This applies to the right-hand Finish and right turns just as well. Therefore, I use "Close" for the left-hand Finish and left turns, and "Heel" for the right-hand Finish and the right turns. To simplify matters for the dog, the statics are broken down into several steps.

STEP ONE

Sit the dog and twizzle to the Heel position. Tell the dog to sit, take one step forward and make a quarter (90-degree) turn to the left. Simultaneously step back with the left leg, give the dog the Close command and guide him back, using the left hand as a funnel for the lead.

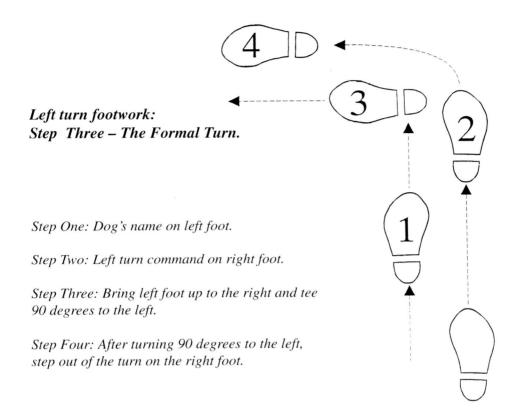

Left turn footwork:
Step Three – The Formal Turn.

Step One: Dog's name on left foot.

Step Two: Left turn command on right foot.

Step Three: Bring left foot up to the right and tee 90 degrees to the left.

Step Four: After turning 90 degrees to the left, step out of the turn on the right foot.

Once the dog is back by the left leg, praise him, and pause for a second or two with the dog back by the left leg. Then close the left leg up to the right, repeating the Close command.

This step is two separate movements, taking the dog back to the left leg, and then closing the left leg up to the right. Do not make the mistake of making it one continuous movement. The priority at this moment is teaching the dog to move back to close up to the left leg, not to sit correctly at Heel, which has already been taught. The praise should be given as the dog closes up to the left leg – which is the new step – finishing off by closing up left to right is not our priority. If we make the mistake of making this one continuous movement, the dog will learn to curve round in a half circle to sit at Heel, whereas we want him to go straight back and then straight forward after the pause, in two legs of a triangle instead of a half circle. If you find that the dog finds it difficult to go far enough back and attempts to position himself in front of the left leg, finish off by taking your right leg back to close up to the left, which will discourage the dog from forward movement.

When first teaching this step, you will find it necessary to look at the dog as he is closing up. Do not worry about this for the first few times, just concentrate on making sure that the dog does it correctly. Once this is the case, carry on teaching while making sure that your eyes are positioned so that you are looking at the ground a yard or two ahead of you, and that your body is as upright as possible to avoid a shoulder command. When you are using the lead, make sure your left arm makes a straight line movement backwards followed by a straight line movement forwards, just as you want the dog to do. As the dog begins to understand, gradually remove the lead influence so that the dog understands that he must clue from the body language and verbal command, and only use the lead as a secondary aid.

STEP TWO

This step is very similar to the previous step, with the exception that you sit the dog at Heel and take a step to the right, resulting in both handler and dog facing the same direction. The lead technique and step back are the same as the previous step; in fact, the only difference is the position of the dog. As you teach this step, you must make sure that the dog moves backwards to close up to the left leg. If he attempts to turn around and walk forwards into the Close position, he probably has not understood the first step (or, most probably, you have not understood it), so go back and spend some time making sure that the dog is going straight back to the left leg and not circling. In Step Two, you are teaching the dog to use his back end, and to move simultaneously backwards and sidewards to close up. He should be able to do this without lead help, just by reading your body movement. Once this is so, you can continue.

STEP THREE

In this step, the aim is to teach the dog to turn to the left simultaneously with the left leg. The two previous steps taught him the movement he must make, but the starting point was always with the dog out of the Heel position. In this step, he will, for the first time, make a left turn while in the Heel position.

The first part of this step is exactly the same as in Step Two, with an additional turn joined on as the dog comes into the Heel position. Place the dog at Heel, take a step to the right, and close the dog up as in the previous step. But as you close the left leg up to right, instead of sitting the dog, tee the left foot to the left and make a quarter (90 degree) turn to the left. At the same time, give the dog another Close command, helping him turn with the lead pressure. This is, in fact, three movements: taking the dog back, closing him up to Heel, and then pivoting to the left turn.

As in the previous steps, help the dog as much as needed, but try to reduce the lead influence where possible. As a finished product, you want the dog to be capable of closing into the Heel position and turning to the left, with only the verbal command and our body movement as signals. Once he can do this, you can teach the left turn during Heelwork.

LEFT TURN ON THE MOVE

The left turn on the move is broken down into two separate steps:

STEP ONE

Bearing in mind that the timing of the left turn is imperative, you must now, more than in

Left About Turn Footwork. Method One.

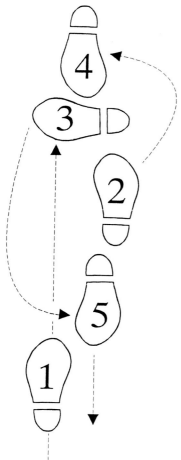

Step One: Dog's name on left foot.

Step Two: Left turn command on right foot.

Step Three: Bring left foot up to the right and tee 90 degrees to the left.
Step Four: Turn right foot 180 degrees and place the toe by the instep of the left foot.

Step Five: Step out of the turn on the left foot.

Left About Turn Footwork. Method Two.

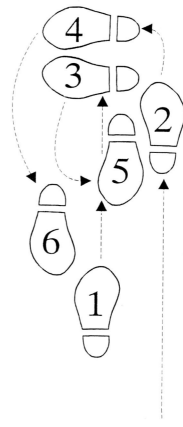

Step One: Dog's name on left foot.

Step Two: Left turn command on right foot.

Step Three: Bring left foot up to the right and tee 90 degrees to the left.

Step Four: Turn right foot 90 degrees and place alongside the left foot.

Step Five: Turn the left foot on the spot 90 degrees to the left.

Step Six: Step out of the turn on the right foot.

any other part of teaching Heelwork, be completely sure that your timing and deportment is absolutely correct. Start off with the dog working correctly at Heel. As your left foot touches the ground, call the dog's name, and as the right foot touches the ground, give the Close command, and *simultaneously,* take the dog back with the lead. While pivoting on your right foot, swing your left foot back in a quarter turn, then close your left leg up to your right. This is quite difficult at first, which is why you must perfect this movement yourself before trying it with the dog.

In this way, the dog will get the left turn signal while the left leg is still back, and as we will not (yet) close the left leg up to the right (as in the formal turn), the dog will follow the body signal to turn left, while at the same time maintaining his position next to the left leg. Once this turn has been completed and the dog is fully turned, you can then close the left leg up to the right and sit the dog. As in teaching the other turns, do not take more than one or two steps out of the turn, as this may distract the dog from concentrating on the turn. Remember to praise the dog in the turn, not afterwards. The praise should come as the dog closes up to the left leg, as you step back in the turn. Pause there for a second or two before carrying on out of the turn.

STEP TWO
Once the dog is closing up confidently in the previous step, you can introduce your formal footwork and deportment, while at the same time stepping back in the turn to keep the dog using his back end. The only difference in this step, from Step One on the move, is that you will close up the left leg to the right before stepping back. At this point, I do not really mind if you step back with the left or the right leg in the turn; I step back on either. It will not make much difference to the dog which leg goes back, but you should decide when training your deportment which leg you will be stepping back on.

The most important part of this step is to give the command "Close" while the left leg is back. Start to turn to the left as you bring the left leg up to the right, placing the left foot on the ground, pointing to the left. Then step back and praise the dog before continuing out of the turn. Be careful about watching your dog into the turn, and if you find that you are doing so, make sure that you wean him off this powerful aid as soon as possible. The dog should be turning either to the left or, for that matter, to the right on your body language, and, needless to say, that body language must also be acceptable to the judge.

STEP THREE
The two previous steps have taught the dog to read left turn body signals, and to tuck in on the left turn. Once the dog understands and can, if required, turn left correctly without the aids, you can, occasionally, do a formal left turn as required in competition. However, as often as not the step back should be incorporated to ensure the tuck in.

LEFT ABOUT-TURNS
Although the left about-turns are only allowed in the higher classes (and not at all in American Obedience), I find it an excellent training step to teach the dog to close up and maintain his position, so I teach it as soon as the dog is confident in the left turn. The left

about-turn is, of course, a double left turn, and the only complicated thing about it is getting your footwork correct, as this determines your balance in the turn. There are several ways of turning and, yet again, you must decide how you are going to turn and become competent before trying to teach the dog.

The timing and commands are the same as for the left turn, with a second command being given as you start the second left turn. Start the turn, as you did for Step Two of the left turn, by placing the left leg up to the right. But instead of stepping back, pivot another 90 degrees to the left while giving the second Close command. The second part of the turn should only be attempted if the dog has maintained his position, and has turned correctly the first 90 degrees. You should also pause for half a beat before completing the second part of the turn. You are, in fact, doing two left turns, which you will gradually turn into one left about-turn. After completing the turn, step back on one leg to ensure that the dog closes up, and praise him for being correct before stepping forward. As with all turns, do not take more than a step or two out of the turn, but stop, praise and release the dog.

PUTTING IT ALL TOGETHER
Once the four basic turns, together with the closing-up exercise have been taught, your daily sessions for training Heelwork have been determined. Each day you can do left circles, right circles, figures and weaves to teach your dog to maintain his position, and to increase his ability to concentrate and pay attention while on the move. You can now incorporate, one turn at a time, all the turns into the twenty steps of Heelwork, together with starts and halts. This will improve precision, and keeping within the twenty steps will ensure that each stretch of Heelwork is short. As the dog improves, you can combine two turns and then three, all within the twenty steps. At first all the turns will be the same, i.e. two right turns or two about-turns. Later on, you can alternate with one left turn, one about-turn and so on, but still restricting the amount of Heelwork to twenty steps. The only time that you do more than twenty steps is in the circles and weaves.

ALTERNATING THE AIDS
We must, at all times, be aware of the aids that we employ to ensure that the dog is working correctly. Once you are sure that the dog is confident and happy, you can start to alternate these aids to avoid the dog becoming addicted to a signal that will cost marks in competition. The aids that we employ to train the dog can be divided into two categories:
1. The *intentional* aids, such as voice, lead and body signals, which are part of the technique used to train the dog. If used as intended, these aids are constantly employed until the dog has been taught an exercise, and are then alternately left off, one at a time, during further training.
2. The *unintentional* aids, such as eye contact, head movement, shoulder signals and so on. These are the aids that are most commonly the cause of the dog working differently in the ring than in training. An example of this is the handler who maintains constant eye contact in training, and then lifts his eyes and looks ahead while competing. Another example is the handler who drops and swings the left shoulder while training the left turn, and then dispenses with this signal in the ring as it would be seen as a blatant extra command.

INTENTIONAL AIDS

Leaving off the intentional aids normally causes no undue problems, simply because the handler is aware that the aids are being used and can therefore alternately leave off the aids that would cost points in competition. For example, when teaching an about-turn my aids would be footwork, lead technique, the dog's name, the command for about-turn, and praise in the turn. In the novice class some of these aids would not be penalised, as extra commands are allowed in the lower classes. Therefore, I would give special attention to alternating the lead technique. In actual fact, I would start to alternate the use of all the aids once the dog was confident in his work, as there is a risk in applying all the aids all the time, because the dog may come to depend on them. Therefore, a typical training session for the about-turn would entail making seven about-turns, each time alternating the aids. I would make the about-turns in this way:

1. Using all the aids.
2. Leave off the lead only.
3. Leave off the dog's name but give the command for the turn.
4. Leave off the command but call the dog's name.
5. Leave off the name and command but praise in the turn.
6. Formal turn, leaving off all the aids except footwork.
7. Using all the aids.

By alternatively leaving off the aids one at a time, the dog will learn to turn without the aids but will actually only make one formal turn in seven. Therefore, he will never learn to make a mistake.

UNINTENTIONAL AIDS

These aids are much more difficult to recognise than the intentional aids. Each handler has a manner of body movement and language that is highly personal and unique. It would be wrong to change this into an unnatural technique. Occasionally, we hear comments about a handler such as "she is a natural" or other similar complimentary remarks. In fact, these handlers have a way of moving that is complementary to their dogs, which is also acceptable within the rules of competition. Most competitors are less fortunate and have (unintentionally) developed two distinct styles of work. In training they bond well with the dog but with a style of movement that would be penalised in competition. Therefore, this must be altered in the ring.

The first step to resolving this problem is to accept that the cause of a dog working differently in the ring than in training lies with (often very subtle) differences in the handler's performance. Once the dog is capable of working without the intentional aids, attention should be given to the unintentional signals. To do this, the handler should work a novice round and ask an experienced instructor to examine the performance and study the handler's deportment from head to toe, and comment on all movements made. This can then be compared to the same round done as a training round. Use of a video can also help.

Bear in mind that body signals and other movements that would be classed as extra commands in the ring are only wrong in training if you are not aware that you are doing them. If you are aware of them, they will fall into the category of intentional aids and can be alternated during training.

FROM NOVICE TO CLASS A

The transition from Novice to Class A often causes problems that can be avoided if the aids are alternated as described. Many handlers make the mistake of interpreting the rules for the Novice Class stating that extra commands *may* be given as extra commands *must* be given. Most handlers enter two classes, Novice and Class A. They then constantly talk and swing about in Novice, only dropping all help in the A class. This can be very traumatic for a young dog. If the dog is working well in Novice, the commands and signals should be alternated in the Novice Class so that the transition to Class A is less defined.

In training, most handlers start off by helping the dog and encouraging him constantly until he is 'warmed up', and then follow this up by endless formal Heelwork, without help. In other words, they start off positively and finish on a negative note. With an advanced dog, I will occasionally start off with a few steps of Heelwork without the intentional aids, and then introduce the aids once the dog has worked 'formally'. In this way the exercise always ends on a positive note while, at the same time, I have simulated the formal start, as in competition. So when preparing for Test A, I start formal and end with all the aids.

In Class A, attention should be given to what help can be given, rather than what is not allowed. A couple of days invested in watching the ticket classes at a Championship show will help the novice handler appreciate that these highly-trained handlers and dogs are communicating constantly with each other while competing, but in a way that is acceptable within the rules of competition.

Chapter Seven

HEELWORK III: ADVANCED WORK

CHANGES OF PACE

I do not teach fast and slow pace until the dog is confident and can maintain a good position in normal pace. Changes of pace should not be attempted from the Halt, nor should any turns be incorporated until the dog is happy and confident while heeling in fast and slow pace.

Lagging and worry caused by lack of confidence are the most common faults found with these exercises. The fact that changes of pace are part of the Class B and C tests often means that handlers think of them as advanced exercises and do not actually train but practise them, mistakenly believing that, as the dog can work at normal pace, he should also be able to work at the fast and slow paces. The secret of teaching happy fast and slow pace lies in accepting the fact that if you have already taught the dog to work correctly at normal pace, you can repeat the same basic steps to teach the dog to do the same thing at a faster or slower pace. When you taught your dog the first steps of Heelwork, you did not start off by heeling for ten minutes or so and expect the dog to understand and be happy. Therefore, it would be wrong to expect him to understand fast or slow pace taught in this way.

By utilising the first steps of teaching Heelwork on the move, starting from Step One and building up to left and right-hand circles, in the same way as we did when introducing the dog to the Heelwork exercise at normal pace, the dog will gradually learn the different paces just as he learnt normal pace. If the method worked once, it will work again.

When teaching normal pace, you started off by backing away from the dog and encouraging him into standing in the Present, at which time you turned into the Heelwork position, and did one step of Heelwork before stopping and praising the dog. Gradually the amount of steps taken were increased, one at a time, to build up into a left-hand circle. Fast and slow pace should be taught in the same way, using all the aids, and speaking to the dog in the same tone of voice.

In normal pace we did not attempt to start Heelwork from the Halt until the dog was happy and confident on the move. The same principles and methods apply to starting fast and slow from the Halt. Needless to say, the turns will be taught in the same way. Therefore, before teaching fast or slow pace, you must ask yourself if you are happy with normal pace. If you are, repeat the same basic method that taught normal pace so well, with the same encouragement and help that was used, and repeat the act at fast and slow pace. Remember at all times to treat the dog as a beginner, as you did when teaching normal pace.

FOOTWORK AND DEPORTMENT

You will most probably have to adapt your footwork slightly for the changes of pace. The size of dog in relation to handler will determine the size of step. Trial and error will determine the right tempo as this is a very personal thing and differs from team to team. Footwork may also need some modification. A dog that performs a correct left turn in normal pace may tend to over-turn in slow pace. This can be avoided by loosening the tee with the left foot, while applying slight lead pressure to ensure that the dog maintains his position. A similar problem applies to the left turns in fast pace, where many handlers have trouble making a tee with the left foot. I find that by stepping very slightly to the right with the right foot and then closing up with the left, I can turn more easily.

Your dog should be working happily and confidently in the correct Heelwork position before you introduce changes of pace.

Fast pace: This should be taught in exactly the same way as for normal pace, approaching the exercise in the same positive manner.

Body movements, such as leaning forward in fast pace, can cause wide work or lagging. I like to compare making turns with riding a bike. There are two ways to make a turn, by turning the handlebars or leaning over. This also applies to making turns in Heelwork at fast pace. If you lean over you will cut the corner, so you have to stay upright and turn the handlebars (your body).

Another common fault is changing the tone of voice to suit the pace. In normal pace, your voice is happy and enthusiastic and should remain so for fast and slow pace. However, many people go 'over the top' in fast pace and then become quiet and serious in slow pace. They then wonder why their dogs react differently in fast and normal.

If you teach fast and slow pace in the same way as you did normal pace, with the same positive attitude, the dog will react in the same way.

ADVANCED STAND, SIT AND DOWN

The Advanced Stand, Sit and Down (ASSD) positions are a 'C only' exercise and should give no undue problems if Distant Control (DC) has been perfected, before attempting to include the ASSD into Heelwork. The commands, given in exactly the same way, are the same as the DC commands, with the same aids being applied.

As with teaching Distant Control, the three positions should be taught one at a time and never included in the Heelwork training until the dog is happy and confident. The sequence of teaching the positions is a matter of personal preference. I normally begin with the Sit position which the dog already knows in Heelwork and is, therefore, perhaps the easiest to start off with. In Distant Control we used a combination of commands and body signals to teach the dog the positions, and we can now make use of these signals when teaching the ASSD.

THE SIT: I use the verbal command in combination with the right foot instep as signal, together with the lead in the left hand.

THE STAND: I use the dog's name and command, together with a left-hand signal (this will be new to the dog and will replace the verbal command once the dog is confident). I also use the left foot under the dog's body to prevent the dog trying to sit.. I use a verbal command together with the left foot, as in teaching DC, to ensure a quick response.

With each position I give the relevant command as I stop, while applying the aids. I then praise the dog and circle around him before praising once again and releasing. As the dog becomes confident, I lengthen the circle around the dog into an oval and eventually into a straight line. With an experienced dog, I give the command and apply the aids, turn and walk backwards to the end of the lead, then walk back past the dog, turn again and collect him, before praising and releasing him. Even with very experienced dogs, I continually praise and encourage as I walk to the end of the lead. In this way, the dog has no opportunity to miss a position or paddle forward.

I prefer to walk at a tempo slightly slower than normal pace when teaching the positions, as this allows me more time to apply the aids.

THE SIT
Heel the dog for a few steps and encourage him by saying "Ready, steady" or such like. As your left leg comes up to the right, give the Sit command, and take the lead, held in your left hand, back behind the dog. As the dog sits, turn in front of him and place the instep of your right foot in front of his paws. Praise him for sitting, then circle around him, making sure that he does not move. Then praise and release him.

THE DOWN
With the lead held in the left hand, heel the dog for a few steps and as the right foot is forward and on the ground, give the dog the Down command and close the left leg up to right, raising the foot to signal the dog to go down as in the Distant Control exercise. If the dog is slow to respond, the left foot can be placed on the lead and the dog can be *gently* pulled into the Down position. Praise the dog for going down, and then finish off the

exercise in the same way as the Sit. However, make sure that the dog does not try to come up into the Sit position as you return to Heel.

THE STAND
Walk with the dog at Heel as before. As the right leg comes forward past the left, give the dog the Stand command, transfer your weight on to your right leg, then place your left leg, toe down, under the dog's tummy. The lead, held in your left hand, can be carefully pulled backwards over the back of the dog (not vertically) to prevent forward movement. Do not try to lift the dog with your left foot. If the dog stands as required, he will feel no contact with the foot. If he tries to sit, the foot under his tummy will prevent him from doing so.

As the dog becomes confident, the lead can be transferred to the right hand and the left hand signal can be introduced.

Once the dog becomes proficient in each position, the circle around the dog can be elongated into a straight line, as described. When first attempting the position, it may be necessary to stop before applying the aids. This will not create any undue problems, so long as you are aware that you are doing it and stop doing so as your technique improves. The same principle applies to other body signals, such as eye contact or shoulder movement. They are only a fault if you are unaware of them.

Once the dog has been taught the advanced positions, they can occasionally be incorporated into his Heelwork training. However, as a rule, they should be trained every day as a separate exercise to maintain precision and enthusiasm.

Chapter Eight

TEACHING RECALLS

THE NOVICE RECALL

The Novice Recall is an exercise that can be found in every class, as an independent exercise in Pre-Beginners, Beginners and Novice, and is incorporated in the Retrieve and in Scent Discrimination from Beginners through to Class C. With this in mind, it must be obvious that a fast, correct Recall is paramount to success in Competition Obedience. Furthermore, the Novice Recall should be taught and perfected before attempting to teach the formal Retrieve and Scent exercises. If not, any Recall faults will be reproduced in these two exercises.

Prior to teaching the formal exercise, you can prepare the dog by teaching him that coming to you is fun. You can also lay the groundwork for correct Presents long before you demand the formal exercise.

DEVELOPING THE FAST RETURN

This can be taught equally well to a puppy or to an adult dog, with only slight adaptation depending on the size of the dog. With young puppies, sit on the ground with your legs spread out to form a 'V', which will help guide the puppy into position. With larger dogs, you will need to get down on your knees with your bottom resting on your heels. With large dogs, you can make use of a bar-stool, and lean back with your legs placed slightly out in front.

To teach this, you will need a family member or a friend to assist. Get the helper to hold the dog by the collar while you are standing in front of the dog, show the dog the reward (food is preferable to toys, but either will do), and then back away about ten yards and position yourself, as described, according to the size of your dog. Call the dog and encourage him to come to you with a happy and exciting voice. Once you see that the dog *wants* to come and is excited, let the helper hold the dog for a second or two longer before releasing the dog. Call the dog to you and make a great fuss of him before giving him his reward. Do not insist on a Sit in the Present, just guide the dog in with your hands and reward him for coming.

Take the dog back to the helper, or let the helper come and get the dog and take him back to the starting point, and repeat four or five times. If the helper is someone the dog knows well, then the helper can also position himself to call the dog and the dog can be called to and fro, each person playing alternately as caller and assistant. Even very young puppies will learn quickly that this is a great game and lots of fun. The ability to 'read' the dog and to release him only when he is excited is extremely important, as is the choice of reward.

THE CHAIR

Sit in a chair and position your feet according to the size of your dog, so that your feet will guide the dog into the Present. Put the dog on the lead and tempt (with a tidbit or a toy) into a Sit anywhere within a half circle at arm's length. Give the Recall command, guide the dog to move to a position directly in front of you, and then guide him between your legs into the Present. Praise him for presenting, then repeat from a different starting point. In this way, the dog can be called from any angle within a 180 degree radius into a straight Present. With

A chair or a stool can be used with a larger dog in order to teach a correct Present.

larger dogs, a bar-stool may be more suitable. Later on, when the formal Recall is being taught and the dog can sit and wait, you can leave the dog and then sit in the chair before calling him, in this way always guaranteeing a straight Present. Gradually decrease the hand help until the dog will Present on Recall command only. This is, of course, the ideal way to introduce angled Presents.

PREPARING THE PRESENT
Using the same principle as when teaching the dog the Heel position, place the dog in the Sit and position yourself in the Present, then praise the dog for sitting correctly before releasing him. By repeating this exercise regularly, the dog will learn his position in the Sit prior to being called into the Present.

TEACHING THE FORMAL EXERCISE
The Novice Recall is in fact four separate exercises:

1. The Sit.
2. The Wait.
3. The Recall.
4. The Present.

I have purposely excluded the left and right-hand Finishes, which will be handled later in the chapter.

The four exercises that make up the Novice Recall have been listed in the order that they are performed in the ring. However, you can teach the exercises in any order, depending on the progress made in similar, related exercises and the age of the dog.

THE SIT AND WAIT
The Sit exercise should already be well-established through teaching the dog Steps Two and Three of Attention training, and you may be well along the road in teaching the Sit-stay exercise. If the Sit-stay has not been taught, then you should leave the Sit and the Wait until such time as the Sit-stay is established to avoid confusion. If this is the case, you can still start to teach Step Three, the Recall, which will be explained later.

Presuming the Sit-stay has been taught and the dog is happy and confident, you can start to teach the Wait.

Place the dog in the Sit position, yourself in the Present, and then twizzle into the Heel position, as in Step Three of Attention training. Tell the dog to sit and stepping off on the right leg (body language for stay sitting), leave the dog and walk to the end of the lead. Turn and face the dog and praise him for sitting. Wait for a second or two at the end of the lead, continually praising the dog, then return to the dog and position yourself in the Present position, so that the dog is sitting perfectly straight and correct. Praise the dog once again before completing another turn into the Heel position. Praise the dog once again and then release him.

This step should be repeated three or four times before attempting to call the dog.

However, before describing what comes next, it is worth taking time to think about what you have just achieved both from your point of view and from that of the dog. All you have asked from the dog is that he sits on command and pays attention, which he already knows how to do from Step Two of Attention training. You have then placed yourself in the Present, thereby ensuring that the dog is sitting straight, because he only has to sit still and co-operate. You then made a turn into the Heelwork position which, once again, the dog knows from Step Three of Attention training. Next, you commanded the dog to sit, walked to the end of the lead and turned to face the dog, which is what you are teaching at this point. You then returned to the Present and then completed another turn to the Heel position. During this whole exercise, the dog only had to sit and co-operate.

You introduced the Wait step to the dog while, at the same time, having a bonus of two Presents and two Sits at Heel, all of which the dog did correctly, as you positioned yourself to the dog and not vice versa. By repeating this Wait step three or four times prior to calling the dog, you will avoid anticipation. In this way, when you eventually call the dog into the Present, he will already have an idea of where and how he must sit.

THE RECALL

Start off by repeating the Sit and the Wait steps, described previously, three or four times. Leave the dog as before and walk to the end of a loose lead. There should be just enough slack in the lead so that when the hands are held at your sides, the lead is not taut. You must now do three things simultaneously: call the dog, take one step back, and bring your hands into your groin. This will have the effect of flicking the lead, if the dog does not react immediately. Once the dog is moving, continue backwards until the dog catches up with you, and then stop so that the dog can present.

Many handlers make the mistake of continuing to back away once the dog has reached them. This actually causes the dog to slow down, because the dog's speed combined with the speed that the handler backs away, determines the Recall speed. Once the dog has caught up, he can only walk at the handler's speed and so has to slow down.

Once the dog has reached the Present position, praise him and then either turn to Heel or release the dog from the Present. Once the dog is running in quickly, it should not be necessary to back away every time while calling the dog. The voice command and flick on the lead will be all that is needed to encourage the dog to come quickly into the Present.

Bear in mind that we are teaching the Recall and not the Present at this time, therefore the Present is not a priority. It would be wrong to slow up a fast Recall by insisting on a correct Present, which is taught as a separate exercise.

THE PRESENT

Place the dog in the Sit and position yourself in the Present with your hands giving the Present command. Take a step back with one leg at the same time calling the dog. Close up with the other leg while giving the dog the Sit command. Praise the dog for presenting before repeating the same movement. Remember to praise the dog each time for presenting before repeating.

By adjusting the size of the step backwards, the dog will not have the room to stand up and walk into the Present and instead will learn to 'bunny-hop' from one Sit to another. In this way the dog will learn to tuck his bottom into the Present and not rock backwards. This will also ensure that the dog starts to sit while moving forward, which is essential for straight Sits. Crooked Sits are as often as not caused by the dog first stopping before attempting to sit. Teaching the 'bunny-hop' precludes this.

Once the dog has been taught the straight Present, you can commence to teach angled Presents, which will be needed for the Retrieve and Scent exercises.

RIGHT-ANGLED PRESENT

Sit the dog and position yourself in the Present. Take one step back and then one step to the left, with the lead in your right hand. Step back with the left leg only and call the dog in, while guiding him to the left, until he is straight in front before guiding him further into the Present. Make two distinct movements with the hands to guide the dog in, first to straighten him up in front by moving him to the left, and then to guide him around the right leg into the Present. As the dog straightens up in front, close the right leg up to the left. Praise the dog for a correct Present, then release.

LEFT-ANGLED PRESENT

Sit the dog and position yourself in the Present, just as for the right-angled Present. Take one step back and then one step to the right, with the lead in your left hand. Step back with the right leg only, and guide the dog into the Present as with the right-angled Present. Step back, with the left leg closing up to the right, as the dog presents. Praise and release as before.

You can gradually increase the angle from left or right by taking a smaller step back and a larger step to either left or right, until such time as the step back is no longer required.

PREPARING THE RETRIEVE

Once the dog has been taught to hold a dumb-bell and a cloth, you can repeat all of the above steps while the dog is holding his retrieve-article, thereby ensuring that the dog does not react differently during the Recall if he has something in his mouth.

THE FINISH

The Finish is the only exercise in Obedience where the handler may make a choice as to how the exercise is performed. In the right-hand Finish the dog must circle behind the handler to sit at Heel, and in the left-hand or Continental Finish, as it was earlier called, the dog must pivot to the left of the handler to finish at Heel.

If you look a little closer at how the dog must move to perform these two exercises, you can see that the movement for both the left-hand and right-hand Finish is very similar to the movement he must make in the left and right (about) turns. For this reason, I prefer to use the same commands, i.e. the left-hand Finish and the left turns are "Close", while the right-hand Finish and the right turns are "Heel". I always teach both Finishes so that later I can command the dog either way, which may help in preventing anticipation as the dog does not know which command will be coming. In training, I never combine a Finish from the formal Present after a Recall, Retrieve, or Scent exercise for the same reason.

Once the dog has been taught both the Present and both Finishes, I will finish off in four different ways, either releasing the dog in the Present, twizzle to Heel myself, step to the right and let the dog do a left-hand Finish, or step to the left and let the dog do a right-hand Finish. If I want to train the formal Finish, it is done as a separate exercise, never combined with a Recall and (formal) Present, as in the ring.

RIGHT-HAND FINISH

STEP ONE
Place the dog in the Sit and position yourself in the Present. Take one step to the left so that the dog is sitting just to the right of your right leg in an off-centred Present. Place the lead around the back of your legs into the left hand. The first few times you may need to use your right hand just under the dog's chin in the collar to get the dog moving. Give the dog the Heel command, and gently guide the dog with the right hand behind your legs. The moment that the dog is moving, the right hand is removed from the collar and the left hand takes over the gentle pressure to pull the dog round into the Heel position. As the dog comes into the Heel position, place him in the Sit.

If your dog is one of the larger breeds, it may be necessary to take a step forward with the right leg and then close up left to right as the dog comes into the Heel position, to give the dog enough room to sit straight at Heel. Repeat this step until the right-hand tug to start the dog moving is no longer needed, and the left-hand lead pressure is almost non-existent and is only used if the dog does not react immediately to the voice command. If you prefer to use an arm signal to finish the dog, then this should be introduced once the dog is happy and confident in this step and should always be used together with his name and a verbal command in training.

STEP TWO
This step is very similar to Step One, with the only difference being the use of the lead. In Step Two the lead will be held in the left hand, which is placed approximately on your midriff with the lead hanging loosely down in front to the dog, who is sitting in the off-centred Present as in Step One. The dog is commanded to go to Heel and as he turns around the back of the legs, the lead will follow him round and tighten as he comes into the Heel position. This will result in the dog completing a tight, correct Finish and will prevent a forward Sit at Heel.

It will be obvious that the correct length of lead is paramount to success. If the lead is too short, the dog will do a backward Sit; if it is too long, you will give the dog room to sit forward or wide. To assess the correct length of lead needed, place the dog at Heel and feed the lead behind your legs into your left hand, held at your midriff. Now, tighten up the lead so that it is just tight. This is the correct length of lead needed in this step.

This step in extremely important with keen Retrieve dogs that tend to sit forward in the Heel position in an attempt to keep an eye on the retrieve-article. To prevent this, train this step while holding a toy or retrieve-article in the left hand, thereby teaching the dog to go to Heel correctly even under distraction.

THE RIGHT-HAND FINISH: STEP ONE

Position yourself in the Present and then take one step to the left. Take the lead around and behind your legs and into the left hand.

The correct lead position for Step One, viewed from the front.

THE RIGHT-HAND FINISH: STEP TWO

Position yourself as in Step One, but this time hold the lead in your left hand, and allow it to hang loosely in front of the dog.

The dog is called into the Heel position and placed in the Sit. Note the position of the lead.

LEFT-HAND FINISH
This exercise is taught in three steps. Initially, bending over the dog and dropping the left shoulder will be unavoidable when teaching this exercise. However, as long as you realise that this could become the signal for the dog to close up, and consciously remove the body signal once the dog is confident, no harm will be done.

STEP ONE
In this step the dog will learn to pivot on his front end and circle with his back legs on command, coming from behind the left leg into the Heel position. Place the dog in the Sit, walk past the right-hand side of the dog and position yourself behind and slightly to the right of the dog, while facing the opposite way. Give the dog the Attention command, "Watch", and ensure that he is watching you over his left shoulder. Give the dog the Close command, and flick the lead to encourage him to move. As the dog turns and comes into the Heel position, repeat the Close command and sit him in the Heel position. Praise the dog for closing to Heel and release.

THE LEFT-HAND FINISH: STEP ONE

Place the dog in the Sit and position yourself behind and slightly to the right of the dog. Give the Attention command, and then the command Close, flicking the lead to encourage the dog to come into the Heel position.

THE LEFT-HAND FINISH: STEP TWO

Place the dog in the Sit, take one step forward and make a quarter turn to the left. Holding the lead in your right hand, command the dog and simultaneously step back with the left leg and slide your left hand down the lead to guide the dog back to your left leg, before closing up into the Heel position.

The first few times that this step is done, you will find it is necessary to watch the dog moving into the Heel position. However, as progress is made you must try to keep your body straight and break eye contact, so that as the dog comes into the Heel position, you are not confusing him with exaggerated body movements. It may help to take a step back with the left leg as the dog moves into the Heel position, and then close left leg up to right, as an aid to sitting at Heel. Once the dog has learned to turn and close up to the Heel position without lead help, you can start to teach Step Two. It is worth noting that many dogs insist on watching the handler over the right shoulder in this step. This is caused by the fact that the dogs have been taught to watch from the Heel position, which entails the dog looking up and to the right. If this causes a problem, it may be necessary to start off by positioning yourself more to the left of the dog a few times. Never call the dog to Heel if he is looking over his right shoulder, as he will then turn to the right before closing up.

STEP TWO
Place the dog in the Sit, and position yourself in the Heel position. Command the dog to sit,

take one step forward, and then make a quarter turn to the left. The dog should now be sitting at right angles to you on your left side. The lead will be held in the right hand; the left hand will be used to slide down the lead and guide the dog back behind the left leg, before bringing him forward into the Heel position. Give the dog the Close command, and step back with the left leg while guiding the dog back with the left hand. Praise the dog for closing up, before finishing off by repeating the command "Close", and guiding the dog forward into the Heel position.

As you step make sure that your weight is transferred to your left leg, which will have the effect of taking your body back. If the dog attempts to sit forward of the left leg, do not close up your left leg to the right, but step back closing the right leg back to the left a few times. This will discourage the dog from sitting forward.

Repeat the step until the dog will close up to the left leg without the use of the lead, if you choose not to use it.

STEP THREE

This step is intended to teach the dog to turn on the spot, with his front legs as the centre of the circle, and using his back end to turn into the Heel position. Initially, the dog will have some front end movement; this step helps discourage this, and teaches the dog to use his back end.

Place the dog in the Sit, and position yourself in the Heel position. Command the dog to sit, step around the front of the dog and position yourself with your left leg next to his left shoulder. With the lead held in the right hand, the left hand will be used to slide down the lead and guide the dog back behind the left leg, before guiding him forward into the Heel position. Give the dog the Close command, and using the lead as described, step back with the left leg and guide the dog back. Praise the dog for going back, then repeat the Close command and close the left leg up to right to sit the dog at Heel.

The backward and then forward movements are in themselves two separate steps and should not be made into one complete movement. This would teach the dog to go to Heel, but would not teach him how to use his back end to get there. As in the previous steps, it will be difficult to keep your body straight while teaching this step. Just be aware that excessive body movement will create a bad habit and concentrate on keeping the body as upright as possible, once the dog is confident.

As already mentioned, the steps used to teach the left-hand Finish are similar to the basic static steps used in teaching the left turns and should, therefore, be taught before teaching the left turn on the move.

TEST A RECALL

To teach the Test A Recall, we must combine two things that the dog already knows: the Novice Recall and the Heel position command. Care should be taken only to teach the Test A Recall once the dog is confident and happy in the Novice Recall, in order to avoid confusion.

Place the dog in the Sit and stand in the Heel position. Tell the dog that he is doing Recalls and step off with the right leg to the end of the lead, with your back to the dog. Call the dog

THE LEFT-HAND FINISH: STEP THREE

Position the dog's left shoulder next to your left knee, then step back with the left leg, while applying the lead aid.

into the Heel position and, as he comes into Heel, take a few steps forward and praise him for coming into position before releasing him. It will help to place the left leg back, as the dog comes into the Heel position to guide him in behind before closing left leg up to right. Do not attempt a long stretch of Heelwork, just a few steps to teach the dog to close up on the move is enough to show him what is required.

As the dog improves and understands what you mean, you can walk to the end of the lead and make a turn to the left before calling him in. Then, as progress is made, a turn to the right can be included. These turns should cause little or no problem, as the technique is very similar to teaching the turns as statics.

Once the dog is coming into the Heel position correctly, the lead can be removed to enable you to call the dog from greater distances. I prefer to call the dog while walking in a left, and then later a right-hand circle. These circles can gradually be squared off into left and right turns. However, it is pointless to just walk off and then call the dog to Heel, as in the ring. Leave the dog in the Sit and walk off into a left-hand circle. Keep talking to the dog to encourage him and to keep his attention. As you call him, turn to face him, as you did when teaching the Novice Recall to him as a puppy. Keep walking backwards on the circle, and as the dog reaches you, twizzle into the Heel position and praise him for collecting correctly.

Once the left circle has been taught, the right-hand circle can be used to teach far-side pick-ups and, as with the left circle, this can gradually be straightened into a right turn. By calling the dog while walking a circle, you can increase the difficulty of the pick-up as the dog gains confidence. The easiest pick-up is with the dog sitting at six o'clock. He will be called at three o'clock in the left-hand circle and nine o'clock in the right-hand circle. The most difficult pick-up would then be nine o'clock in the left-hand circle, and three o'clock in the right-hand.

If the dog is running in too quickly and tends to overshoot the leg, try halting the moment that he reaches the leg. However, with proper use of the left leg back method, the dog should learn to collect quickly but to close up from behind, thereby avoiding an overshoot.

I believe that the most common reason for dogs wandering into the Heel position is that the handler tends to approach this exercise with a different attitude than when teaching the Novice Recall. Both are Recalls and both should be taught in an exciting, happy manner. By alternating the Novice and Class A Recalls during training, once the dog is confident in the Novice Recall (and by keeping the same tone of voice and attitude) you will avoid a slow Recall.

Although the Test A Recall forms the basis of the Recall in the Sendaway exercise it is a separate exercise and should always be trained as such. I never combine a Recall and a Sendaway except in the ring.

Chapter Nine

THE RETRIEVE

CHOOSING A METHOD

This exercise is possibly the most controversial of all the exercises taught in Competitive Obedience because there are so many different points of view on how it should be taught. These different points of view can generally be split into two camps: those that advocate the play method and those that prefer the force method. There is also the somewhat smaller group who maintain they have never had to teach the Retrieve by either method because they have had a "natural retriever".

I am not sure that there is such a thing as the natural retriever. I have seen some dogs that will happily and correctly retrieve certain articles, and the owners of these dogs have sworn that they have had no formal training. However, a dog competing in (British) Obedience competitions must retrieve a vast assortment of strange and sometimes awkward articles, and therefore, in my experience, the dog has to be taught to retrieve them. I believe that even the most proficient 'natural retriever' will have his preferences and his dislikes, but our competition dogs must pick up each and every article cleanly, correctly, and without hesitation, as one or two points lost on hesitation or a fumble could make the difference between being a winner or an also-ran.

I have similar reservations regarding the play method, which may be partially successful if the dog is only going to be taught to retrieve a dumb-bell or his own toy. However, I doubt if the play method would succeed in training for competition work, where a dog has to retrieve so many different types of retrieve-articles, many of which he will dislike. Of course, the exception proves the rule, so I am sure that there are some natural retrievers doing well in Obedience, just as there are probably some very successful dogs that have been taught by the play method. However, I often wonder if these dogs have ever refused to retrieve an article, and if so, were made to retrieve it – which is force retrieving by a different name.

If you are training a puppy, and, from the outset, it has been decided that the puppy will be taught to retrieve, then, by the use of play, the basics of the Retrieve exercise can be introduced. This will allow the puppy to associate the Retrieve command with pleasure, and this foundation can be utilised in later training during the first steps of teaching the formal exercise. However, to teach the Retrieve purely by the play method, without any use of force, is extremely difficult for even the most experienced trainer. This is because this method relies almost entirely on the ability of the trainer to understand the thoughts and reactions of the puppy and to be able to react accordingly, and this, sadly, is something that most of us cannot do. Furthermore, the play method is rarely successful with adult dogs, especially if the dog has had prior experience of the Retrieve.

It will have become obvious that my preference in teaching the Retrieve lies with the so-called force method. I object to the word "force" being used and prefer to call this the "taught" method, because there is, in fact, very little physical force involved. As with all dog training, you must repeatedly enforce your will upon the dog, but this applies just as much to Heelwork training as to the Retrieve. Furthermore, I feel that the word "force" may persuade a certain type of person to reject this method because of the name and not because of the method itself. It is important to select a method that will succeed from the start in order to avoid frustration for the trainer and confusion for the dog.

TEACHING THE RETRIEVE

The Retrieve exercise is a combination of five exercises: Sit, Retrieve, Recall, Present, and Finish. It is imperative that the dog is happily and correctly doing the Novice Recall before you attempt to teach a Retrieve. The four steps contained in the Novice Recall will form an integral part of the Retrieve exercise, and any apathy, hesitancy, or technical faults that are not cured before starting on the Retrieve exercise will only be carried forward into the new exercise.

As with all new exercises, everything is taught step by step, each step being thoroughly understood and accepted by the dog before proceeding to the next step. Patience and repetition are the rules, combined with lots of praise. Once again the tone of voice is of ultimate importance; a command is not a threat, nor is it a request. It should be spoken in a positive, no-nonsense but motivating way. Think about how you use your voice when you call your dog to take him for a walk. At that moment you are giving him a command. That same tone of voice should be used for all commands.

As with all new exercises, you are going to need the dog's full attention, therefore you should introduce and teach the exercise in a quiet room with no distractions. Only when the dog is competent in an exercise should he be introduced to the distracting influence of other people or dogs. When introducing the dog to the first steps I prefer not to use a dumb-bell, instead I use a cardboard tube. I have found that the hard cardboard tubes found in fax rolls are ideal.

Before attempting to teach a dog anything, you must be sure in your own mind that you know what you are doing. I find that this can be simplified by setting a general goal, (in this case, teaching the dog to retrieve), then splitting this goal into sections or steps. In turn, you must look at each step to be taught, and be completely aware of what you are attempting to achieve.

For example, in Step One the aim is to teach the dog to quietly and happily sit and hold an article in his mouth, without mouthing, and to do this until he is told to release the article into your hands. If you gently force your will on to the dog, with lots of praise at the right time, the dog will learn quite quickly to accept the article without resentment. It is extremely important that you carry out this (and all teaching) in a positive and confident way, and you can only do this if you are feeling confident and positive. In other words, you must be absolutely sure of what you are doing before you attempt to teach the dog. I always work the step through in my mind until I am confident, before I attempt anything with the dog.

STEP ONE: THE HOLD

Place the dog in the Sit on your left-hand side. The dog does not have to be in the Heel position as long as he is sitting still and is paying attention. With your left hand, using only index finger and thumb, gently encourage the dog to open his mouth by coaxing your finger and thumb into his mouth just behind his canine teeth. As he opens his mouth, place the article into his mouth. Then use only the index finger and thumb of each hand to hold the dog's head up and still. Your left hand should be holding the upper jaw, while your right hand is controlling the lower jaw. Praise the dog and introduce the command "Hold". Do not

Step One: The Hold. Note the use of the hands.

attempt to remove your finger pressure at this stage. All you want to achieve is the dog sitting quietly with the article in his mouth while you encourage and praise him, at the same time introducing the Retrieve command. Let the dog hold the article for only two or three seconds, then give him the Release command and remove the article from his mouth. Repeat this step four or five times and then end the training session.

This sounds all very simple, but for the inexperienced trainer, it is a very difficult step. Many dogs resent having a strange article placed in their mouths and will end up resisting. If this happens, remove the article completely and try to decide what went wrong. Did the dog resent the article, or does he resent the hands? To find out, gently but firmly, open the dog's mouth in the same way as you did when placing the article in his mouth. If the dog accepts his head being held without the article, then his problem is with the article. However, if he fights your hands, you have another problem altogether which you will have to resolve before we can teach the Hold. If the dog accepts your hands, then the problem lies with the article.

For those dogs that resent the hands, all you have to do is gently and gradually introduce the hands over the period of a week or two. Start by placing the two fingers of the left hand over the bridge of the dog's nose for one second, praise the dog for accepting this, and then reward him. Gradually increase the time that the hands are on the dog until he will accept them without resentment. This should only take a week or two at most.

If the dog is accepting the hands but resisting the article, there is no point in getting angry and trying to force the dog to hold the article – this will only lead to more resentment. Just remove the article from the dog's mouth, firmly correct the dog for not sitting still and paying attention, then reintroduce the article, making sure that your attitude is positive and that there is lots of praise. It is extremely important that you do not start correcting the dog for not co-operating while the article is in his mouth. Correction, if needed, should be given with the article removed. In this way, the dog will quickly understand that it is preferable to accept the article in his mouth and be praised than to reject the article and be corrected. Once the dog understands this, he will accept the dumb-bell. You can then increase the length of time that the dog must hold the dumb-bell, while gradually reducing the influence of the hands, until the dog will quietly sit still without mouthing or resenting the article.

By the end of this phase of training, the dog should be happily holding the article and you can give some attention to the Release command. I prefer to take the article with both hands, and I teach the dog that if I have only one hand on the article, he must not release it. I do this by placing one hand on the article and saying "Hold", and then placing the second hand on the article and saying "Leave". I will even give a gentle tug with only one hand on the article while giving the Hold command to encourage the dog to hold firmly.

In the ring, I take the article with two hands but place one hand on the article first, thereby eliminating the risk that the dog will drop the article as I reach for it. From now on, I repeat this two-handed Release every time that I want the dog to release the article. Once this has been achieved, you can start on Step Two.

STEP TWO: THE TAKE
At this stage, the aim is for the dog to quickly take the article on command, from a distance

Step Two: Teaching the dog to take on command.

of only one or two inches in front of his nose. Start off by placing the dog in the Sit on the left-hand side, and gently take hold of his (leather) collar with the middle finger of the left hand. At this point the article is out of sight in the right hand, hidden behind the right leg. Slowly, and with lots of voice encouragement, bring the article into view, all the time watching the dog for a reaction. The moment that the dog looks at the article, hide it as quickly as possible behind the right leg, while, at the same time, restraining the dog from going after the article. It is also very important that the dog is praised in an exciting way the moment he looks at the article.

Keep repeating this 'hide-and-seek' until the dog gets excited, which *all* dogs will do if the tone of voice is right. You are teasing the dog into chasing the article and must therefore praise him for any reaction to the article. Once you see that the dog fully intends to try to take the article, bring it to within an inch or two of his mouth. Simultaneously release the collar pressure and tell the dog to hold. The moment that the article is in his mouth, revert to

Step One and ensure that the dog holds the article for a second or two while you praise him.

The ability to read your dog's reactions is extremely important at this time. The dog must be praised for any reaction whatsoever. Some dogs will try to snatch the first time you do this, others will appear to have no interest at all. If you react correctly so will the dog. It may take a few days of playful teasing to awaken the interest of certain dogs but the instinct is there, you just have to bring it out.

By the end of Step Two, your dog should be sitting and watching the article (which is held two inches in front of his nose) with keen excitement, without actually trying to take it. On hearing the Retrieve command, "Hold", the dog should quickly take the article and then hold it in his mouth until told to release. At this point we can start Step Three.

STEP THREE: THE REACH

Until now, the dog has always been in the Sit, and so now we have to teach him that he can move to take the article. This step should be very easy, in fact all the hard work is over in Steps One and Two.

Step Three:
The dog learns to take
from arm's length.

With the dog sitting on the left-hand side and your left hand in the collar, hold the article in the right hand at arm's length. The dog should by now only have eyes for the article, (if not, go back to Step Two). Excite the dog with your voice until he is raring to go, and then give him the Retrieve command. Keep your control over the dog with your left hand in the collar. As soon as the dog has the article in his mouth, command him to sit and resort to Step One to keep control. You want the dog to sit the moment that the article is in his mouth, so do not let him walk about with the article.

If you have done your work properly, this step should not present any new problems. The only thing that is new is that the dog has had to walk a few steps in order to carry out Step Two, which he already knows. If you do meet with a problem, try to decide whether the problem lies with the dog's attitude or whether it is a technical problem. Whichever it is, the cause of the problem (and therefore the solution) will be found in the first two steps. Do not try to go any further before the problem has been cured.

At this stage I would go back to Step One and re-teach these steps while introducing a dumb-bell as retrieve-article. If you carried on using a fax roll (or whatever) once the dog is retrieving from the ground, you may create the bad habit of teaching the dog to replace the article in his mouth, as certain types of dogs cannot pick up an article that is in contact with the floor without replacing the article in their mouths.

STEP FOUR: AROUND THE ARM

In this step, we want to start to teach the dog to go around the article before picking it up from the far side. To do this, everything is done in the same way as in Step Three, with the exception of how you hold the article. In Step Three the dumb-bell was held at arm's length in front of the dog, with the cross-bar directly in front of the dog. All that you change in Step Four is the position of the dumb-bell, which will now be held on the left side by the thumb and index finger of the right hand, with the rest of the dumb-bell sticking out of the back of the hand. This results in the hand restricting the dog from taking the dumb-bell, except from the far side. In this way, you start to teach the dog to go around the hand and take the dumb-bell from the far side. This has three major advantages:

1. The dog learns self control. A dog that picks up from the far side rarely fumbles a pick-up.
2. A dog taught a far side pick-up sees the handler as he picks up.
3. We have a straight line Recall from the pick-up, as the dog has already turned before the pick-up.

STEP FIVE: AROUND THE LEG

By this time your dog should be extremely happy and confident in the first four steps. It is important to be aware that, until now, the dog has only had to retrieve from the hand, and some dogs may have trouble realising that they can retrieve an article that is not in the hand.

Start off this step with the dog on the left-hand side, placing the dumb-bell on the ground about one foot in front of the dog. Hold the collar lightly in the left hand. Encourage the dog to look at the dumb-bell, and once he is doing so, give him the Retrieve command.

Step Four: Introducing the far side pick-up. The dog goes around the arm to pick up. Note the hand position.

Introducing the dumb-bell: Repeat the first three steps using a dumb-bell.

The dog should now be happy to take the dumb-bell, going round the arm.

Simultaneously, place the left leg to the left of the dumb-bell, thereby forcing the dog to go around the left leg to pick up the dumb-bell from the far side. This should be quite straightforward for a dog that has thoroughly understood and is confident in the previous steps. However, there are two critical points at this stage:

1. If the dog will not look at the dumb-bell on the floor, you cannot give him the Retrieve command. You will have to go back to the previous steps and re-teach, because the dog most probably has an attitude problem that we have missed. He should by now be obsessed with the dumb-bell and if he will not look at it, there is something wrong.

Teaching the dog to mark the article.

2. The transition of retrieving from the hand to the floor is too traumatic, so you will have to gradually remove the hand from the dumb-bell. To do this, crouch down with your hand on the dumb-bell, which is on the floor, and gradually reduce the influence of the hand.

Once the dog realises that he can retrieve from the floor, you can continue to teach Step Five.

As in the previous steps, you want the dog to sit the moment that he has picked up the dumb-bell, but at this stage you want to introduce the Present. You do this by commanding the dog to sit and then positioning yourself in the Present, much as we did when preparing

Step Five: The dog goes around the leg to pick up from the far side.

the dog to Present in the Novice Recall. Do not confuse or worry the dog by insisting that he presents, but you do want to condition him into thinking that, after picking up, the next thing that happens is a Present. By the end of Step Five you should have a dog that is happily and confidently retrieving a dumb-bell that has been placed one foot away on the ground.

STEP SIX: RETRIEVING AT THE END OF A LOOSE LEAD

You can now start to increase the distance the dog has to run out to pick up the dumb-bell. Start by telling the dog to sit, and walk out to the end of the lead. Place the dumb-bell on the ground and stand in front of the dumb-bell, which is about one foot in front of you, with

Step Six: The dog must now learn to run out in order to pick up the dumb-bell.

your back to the dog. With the lead in your left hand, look over your left shoulder and give the dog the Retrieve command. At the same time, give a slight tug on the lead to help the dog to move. Guide the dog to come around to your left, and as he passes your left leg, place the leg past the dumb-bell, as in Step Five. This will ensure that the dog runs out around the dumb-bell and picks up from the far side. The moment that he has completed the pick-up, command him to sit and then position yourself in the Present.

You can now gradually increase the distance the dog has to run by throwing the dumb-bell, then walking out to the end of the lead before commanding the dog to retrieve. The moment the dog moves, run out to the dumb-bell and place your left foot to ensure a far side pick-up. If the dog is too fast, in other words, if you think he will beat you to the dumb-bell, all you have to do is take up the slack on the lead as he goes past you, and physically restrict him from getting to the dumb-bell first. This has the extra advantage of making the dog even quicker. As in the previous steps, you want the dog to sit the moment that he has picked up the dumb-bell. Do not insist that he presents, but position yourself in the correct Present.

COMBINING THE RETRIEVE WITH THE RECALL

You have now taught the dog to quickly and correctly run out and pick up a dumb-bell. All that remains is to incorporate the basic Recall steps in order to teach the dog the formal Retrieve exercise. You can start to do all the Recall steps with the dog holding a dumb-bell, as soon as he is confident in the first three Retrieve steps. In this way the dog is only being taught one new thing at a time. Once the dog can do a Novice Recall, including angled Presents, equally as well with a dumb-bell in his mouth as without, you can start to train the finished article – but always on lead.

Until now you have always (from Step Five onwards) positioned yourself in the Present the moment that the dog has completed the pick-up. So the dog thinks: pick-up, Present, pick-up, Present, with nothing in-between. In training, you never throw the dumb-bell and send the dog out, while you stand still waiting for the dog to return, as he does in competition. If you always break down the exercise into the training steps throughout his life, the dog will be conditioned to present one second after he has picked up, and he will try to present just as quickly in a show situation when we are standing several yards away.

RELEASING THE DUMB-BELL
From Step Five onwards, in other words from the moment the dog picks up from the ground and we start positioning ourselves in the Present, I prefer to tell the dog to release the dumb-bell when I am standing in the Heel position. To teach this, stand in the Present, then twizzle to the left into the Heel position before taking the dumb-bell. In this way, the dog will hold the dumb-bell firmly in his mouth while in the Present. Once again, only take the article while standing in the Present in competition.

By constantly repeating the basic Retrieve and basic Recall steps with the dog holding a dumb-bell, the dog will never get the chance to develop bad habits. Only allow the dog to do a formal Retrieve in the ring. The end result will be a happy, confident and fast retriever.

STRANGE ARTICLES.
You can now proceed to teach the dog to retrieve a variety of articles. Each time you introduce a new type of article, start from Step One and re-teach each step, thereby never allowing the dog to develop bad habits. You will have to introduce hard articles including metal, soft articles, large and small ones, and articles that are awkward to pick up. The list is endless, as is the imagination of most judges! The end result will be an experienced dog that will happily and correctly retrieve anything.

As with any step-by-step method of teaching, it is important to understand and remember what you are trying to teach in each step. Therefore, I have listed the most important lesson to be taught in each step.

STEP ONE: Teaches the dog to hold the dumb-bell correctly without resenting the article or mouthing.

STEP TWO: Teaches the dog to take the article quickly and correctly on command and instils steadiness.

STEP THREE: Teaches the dog to move forward on command to take the dumb-bell. Until now he had only to take from the Sit.

STEP FOUR: Introduces the far side pick-up and teaches the dog self control, as he would prefer to pick up his way but is taught to do it your way.

STEP FIVE: Teaches the dog to pick up from the ground while instilling the far side pick-up. You also start to condition the dog that the Present immediately follows the pick-up.

STEP SIX: Teaches the dog to run out and pick up from the far side. The dumb-bell is also thrown for the first time. By walking out to the dumb-bell before calling the dog, you will instil steadiness.

By constantly repeating these steps and by remembering why you do them, you will prevent any bad habits from developing.

Chapter Ten

THE STAY EXERCISES

CONFRONTING PROBLEMS

For competition purposes, we must teach the dog three different Stay positions and the commands: "Sit", "Stand", and "Down". We also have to give the dog enough confidence so that he will do the Sit and Down exercises while we are out of sight. I believe that there are several reasons that the dog breaks a Stay exercise:

1. Fear of being left behind when the handler leaves.
2. Fear of surroundings.
3. Previous bad experience in the Stay exercises.
4. Lack of concentration during the exercise.
5. Distraction.
6. Physical problems or pain.

At this point many of you will have thought of several other instances of the reason a dog broke his Stay, which do not fall into one of the above-mentioned categories. But, in general, a dog that is not distracted through fear or curiosity about his surroundings, and has the trust that his handler will return to him, will happily do the Stay exercises.

FEAR OF BEING LEFT BEHIND

One of the problems with building a close relationship with a dog is that they often hate being parted from their handler. German Shepherds are notorious for being 'weak' Stay dogs. As often as not, dogs that follow their handlers out of the ring do so because they are not convinced that the handler will *always* come back. This problem will never develop if sound basic Stays are properly taught from the outset.

FEAR OF SURROUNDINGS

A dog that breaks Stays because he is worried or frightened by his surroundings is only reacting in a natural way to one of nature's basic instincts – survival. The correct way to cure this problem is to desensitise the dog from the source of his fear. The first step in doing this is to diagnose the source of the fear. If a dog stays while the handler is in sight but breaks when the handler goes out of sight, then, more often than not, the problem is not fear of surroundings but fear of being left behind.

PREVIOUS BAD EXPERIENCE DURING THE STAY EXERCISE
With the best care in the world, we cannot foresee every eventuality. Dogs fighting, thunderstorms, rain, sudden noises, insects, the list of potential bad experiences is endless. Once a dog has had a traumatic experience in the Stay exercise, you may be confronted with a problem that is extremely difficult and, (very) occasionally, impossible to cure.

LACK OF CONCENTRATION DURING THE EXERCISE.
This problem often manifests itself in the dog that stays in place, but goes to the Sit from the Stand, or to the Down in the Sit-stay. This is normally caused by bad training and, luckily, it is normally easy to cure. A dog that does the opposite, i.e. goes to the Stand from the Sit, or Sit from the Down, normally has another reason, often based on lack of confidence.

DISTRACTION
This type of problem can be seen in the dogs that break the Stay and go and sniff the next dog, or jump up if they see a dog doing Sendaways or Retrieves in the adjacent ring. This sort of problem is, again, easily cured with sound basic training.

PHYSICAL PROBLEMS OR PAIN
A dog that suddenly starts breaking a Stay exercise for no apparent reason may be in pain. Try sitting on the ground or standing perfectly still for two or three minutes, and any old injury or bruise will start to hurt. Our dogs may have minor aches and pains without giving any sign of suffering. If your dog starts breaking a Stay that he has previously done without problem, it may be worthwhile to let him be checked over by your vet.

It should by now have become obvious that we must first of all ascertain the cause of the Stay problem before we can hope to find a solution. With the exception of physical problems or pain, all of the above problems can be cured with sound basic (re)training.

TEACHING THE STAY
In all the Stay exercises we are teaching the dog two things: to stay, and to maintain a certain position. With this in mind, I prefer to teach the dog to stay in one position only, (the Down), until he is happy and confident at being left alone. Once he has learnt to stay happily, I will proceed to teach him the Stays in the other two positions. I prefer to teach the Down-stay first because it is the most relaxed position for the dog. I do not have to fuss or worry about the dog moving one leg or fidgeting about, as with the Sit or Stand, and so I can concentrate on the dog staying.

Prior to teaching the Stays, you will, of course, have taught the dog to sit, stand and lie down, and so you only need to prolong the duration of the exercise to teach the Stay exercises. It is worth mentioning that I prefer not to use the command "Stay" for the Stay exercises – it could confuse the dog, as he will hear the same command for three different exercises. I am not saying that this is wrong, after all, thousands of dogs have been taught with the use of the Stay command. I simply believe that if the dog understands the commands that we use for Sit, Stand, and Down, and also understands that he must keep that position until released, the Stay command becomes unnecessary and potentially confusing.

THE DOWN-STAY

Place the dog in the Down position, which may be either lying flat on his side or lying with the head up but on one flank. I would not allow the dog to do the Down-stay in the 'lion stance' as this is unstable and encourages creeping forward. It is also the preferred position for Distant Control and can, therefore, be confusing. I teach the dog to lie flat with his head on the ground, because he then has to make three movements to come up into the Stand. Whichever position you choose, make sure that the dog always lies in that position and do not allow him to change positions.

Start off by placing the dog in the Down position and crouch down next to him, giving him quiet encouragement and praise. Let him stay in that position for about ten to fifteen seconds. If the dog struggles or tries to get up, do not try to physically hold him down. Let him come out of the Down and then, quietly but firmly, correct him for disobeying the Down command. The correction should be firm enough to subdue the dog without frightening him. Once you get the required submission, praise the dog to show you are not angry, release him, then put him back into the Down position. One or two corrections should be more than enough for even the most boisterous dog.

If the dog has struggled and been reprimanded, you should concentrate on releasing him the moment he co-operates even if he has only been in the Down for a few seconds. Gradually increase the time of the Stay until the dog will quietly stay down for about one minute. Do not try to stand up until the dog is confident and lying still for one minute. You can now place the dog in the Down and stand up straight for a second or two before crouching back down. Once again, gradually increase the amount of time that you stand up. Do not forget to continually encourage and praise the dog; let him know that he is doing right.

The time has now come to take a step away from the dog. We do this by stepping off on the right leg and immediately turning to face him. There is no point in standing with your back to the dog, you must communicate with voice and body language what you want, and you cannot do that if you have your back to him. After taking one step away, return to the dog, crouch down and pet him before releasing him. From now on, you can gradually increase the number of steps you take away from the dog until you can take up to about ten steps, always walking backwards, and continually talking and encouraging the dog. Do not stand still, but continually keep on the move - leaving the dog and going back to him. In a typical one-minute Stay, you may have left and gone back seven or eight times. This convinces the dog that you will always come back and will give him the confidence to stay.

At this point, I start to incorporate the 'ceremony' of circling the dog prior to departure, and repeating this circle prior to releasing him after the command "End of exercise". By doing this, the dog will learn that if we circle him he has got to stay until we return. This circle will also prevent anticipation of the Release as we return.

Gradually you can increase the length of the Down-stay to about two minutes, but always talking and encouraging the dog, walking to and fro, with as much time spent standing or crouching next to him as away from him. The duration of the Stay should constantly vary, lots of short Stays being preferable to one long Stay. Once the dog is happily staying in the Down position, you can start to teach the Stand and Sit-stays.

THE SIT-STAY

The Sit is an integral part of every exercise, except the other Stay exercises and the Temperament Test. Therefore, in teaching the Sit-stay you will be combining two exercises: the Sit that the dog already knows, and the Stay which was taught in the Down position. All worry about being left in the Stay should have been removed in the Down-stay.

The circle ceremony, taught in the Down-stay, will tell the dog that he must stay, and the Sit command will tell him in which position. Apart from the different position, the build-up to the finished exercise is the same as for the Down position – with the exception that you do not have to crouch down prior to leaving the dog. The only other difference is to continually repeat the Sit command, together with praise and encouragement, instead of giving the Down command. I believe that to repeat the stay command could cause confusion at this stage.

Because the Sit is used as the starting point of so many other exercises, you must be more aware of possible confusion with the initial steps of the Stay exercise and make sure your body language does not tell the dog that he must come to you.

THE STAND-STAY

The Stand position is also to be found in the Temperament Test and in Distant Control. The command for the Stand-stay may be the same as for the Temperament Test, but the Stand command in Distant Control should be different. The build-up for the Stand-stay is the same as for the Sit and Down-stays. However, do not be in a hurry to leave your dog. You know that the dog can stay; he has proved that in the other two Stay exercises. He must now learn that he can stand still for one minute, and this is more difficult than it seems.

The Stand is a dominant position, and any dogs that feel even the slightest hesitation or lack of confidence will have the tendency to either sit or lie down. Any correction from the handler that even suggests anger will result in the dog trying to show submission by sitting or lying down. For this reason, most of your Stand-stay training must be done next to the dog or, at most, a step or two away, continually moving and praising and encouraging the dog. Bear in mind, you know that the dog can stay, so you only have to teach him that he can stand for one minute. The build-up for the Stand-stay is the same as for the Sit and the Down, with the emphasis on staying close to the dog until he is confident and happy.

OUT-OF-SIGHT

Most problems with the Stay exercises start when the time comes to train out-of-sight Stays. The golden rule is *never* to do out-of-sight Stays. You may, very occasionally, be out of the dog's sight, but the dog must always be within your sight. As a rule, train the basic steps, as described above, by staying in plain view of the dog. Praising and encouraging the dog for doing right will build his confidence. Occasionally, you can walk out of his sight for a second or two, praising him while out of his sight, then returning into plain view. However, you must never lose sight of the dog.

With a little imagination and planning, you will be able to find a place where you can see the dog without the dog seeing you. Five or ten seconds out of sight, while talking to the dog, is more than enough time to prove to the dog that you are still close by, even if he cannot see you. If you make a habit of going out of sight, the worried dog will start to fret and may break Stays, and the confident dog will get bored, with the same possible results.

GROUP STAYS

Stays are the only exercise that the dog must do simultaneously with other dogs. Do not be tempted to try to teach an inexperienced dog the Stay exercises among other strange dogs. Once your dog is confidently staying at home, join in the Stay exercises at your training club, but stay close to your dog until you are sure that he is not distracted or worried by the other dogs. Always try to sit your dog between dogs that he already knows, and avoid dogs with known Stay problems. The first few times that you attend a show, place your dog outside the ring of the Advanced Stay classes, and practise the Stay exercises with the advanced dogs with your dog on the lead.

If problems develop with a dog that has previously been good in the Stays, try to observe him and attempt to find out the reason for the problem before correcting him. Finding the reason is the first step to curing the problem.

THE TEMPERAMENT TEST

I openly admit that I find the Temperament Test (referred to in the Stand-stay exercise) a silly and useless exercise in its present form. If the test was introduced to test the temperament of Obedience dogs, then it has failed. However as the saying goes: "Ours is not to reason why....".

A well-socialised dog should have little problem with the test. If the dog will accept or is taught to accept being touched by a stranger, and has also been taught to stand still, the test will cause no problems. In training classes, I encourage handlers to let their dogs be petted by other people in the class. This is not done during the lessons but before or after, and it is very informal. The dog should learn that the world is full of friendly people. If I see a dog that seems a bit worried, I get the whole class to offer it a piece of food, without trying to touch it in any way. Most dogs will soon come out of their shell with this sort of treatment. Occasionally, we come across a dog that, for whatever reason, is shy or even outright frightened of being touched, and after weeks of receiving tidbits from other people, remains fearful. This type of dog can still be taught to accept the touch of a judge's hands during the Temperament Test, however he may never learn to enjoy it.

I start off by teaching the dog to stand still, and I then proceed to touch the dog as the judge would. First of all I approach him from the front, then from either side and, last of all, from the rear, gradually teaching the dog to stand still and quietly accept being touched. I then ask a good friend, that the dog knows well and likes, to gently pass his hand over the dog's back. I will then ask yet another friend to help, and so on, until the dog learns to stand still while being touched. As the dog gains confidence, I will use someone that the dog sees only now and then, perhaps at training classes. The last stage of training is to ask a stranger to the dog, but someone you respect and who knows dogs, to perform the test. At the average show, the test can be done many times as most fellow competitors will be more than willing to help.

Most judges will be very careful in conducting the Temperament Test and will approach from the front. However, the occasional judge will try to handle the dog while still holding their clipboard so it is worthwhile training for this sort of situation.

The only exception to the rule is the potentially dangerous dog, who may, through fear or aggression, bite the judge. Once again, by careful training, this type of dog can be trained to accept being touched by a stranger. However, any handler who thinks that their dog may bite should warn the judge beforehand. If the problem is extreme and there is a danger of the judge being attacked, then the dog should not be entered for competitions until the problem has been cured. Thankfully, such dogs are few and far between.

Chapter Eleven

THE SENDAWAY

UNDERSTANDING THE EXERCISE

For competition purposes we want to teach the dog to run out in a straight line for anything up to 50 yards (often much shorter), and then to go down on command. Why, then, should this exercise cause so much confusion? I can only assume it is because the handler does not understand how simple the Sendaway is to teach, thereby making it much more complicated than it needs to be. In modern Obedience competitions we are actually teaching the dog to 'go to' rather than a 'send away', and if we accept this we are halfway to understanding how to teach the dog the exercises.

Looking outside the confines of Competitive Obedience at Sheepdog Trials, the handlers are, in fact, teaching their dogs a go to. The dogs are sent *to* the sheep. A shepherd would never dream of sending his dog a mile or more over the hillside if there were no sheep there, and as the sheep are the dog's reward for obeying the shepherd's command, the result is a fast, correct outrun or Sendaway. Herein lies the secret of a good Obedience Sendaway, always send the dog to his reward and never 'lie' to him by sending him to nothing. Just as a sheepdog is motivated and rewarded by finding the sheep, the Obedience dog can be motivated and rewarded by his toy or food when running out to where you have placed his reward.

A sheepdog will obey the shepherd and run out to the sheep, even if they are out of sight, because the sheep are always where the shepherd says they are. In the same way, Obedience dogs should learn that the reward is always where the handler says it is, i.e. at the end of a straight line. Once the dog has been taught this, he will always do a fast, correct Sendaway. In actual fact when we give the command "Away" we are saying to the dog: "Go, get your reward".

THE REWARD

As in all the other exercises, you must first decide what type of reward to give to the dog – will it be food or a toy? Most importantly, it has to be something that the dog wants. If you decide to use food as the reward, you must make a habit of placing the food on a small, flat saucer or such-like – something that will discourage the dog from searching for food on the ground, but which is invisible from the starting point. Likewise with a toy, you are restricted over the size of the toy as it should also be invisible to the dog from the starting point. Many people use a mat, which is invisible from a distance. However, if the dog plays with the mat, the chances are that he will try to go down next to, instead of on the mat because he sees it as a toy. I use a mat with my dog Woolie, but I have taught him that he must lie on it before he can play with it.

STAGES OF TRAINING

STEP ONE
Place the dog in the Sit and walk out to the place that you want to send the dog to. Crouch down to the ground, sidewards on to the dog (to avoid confusion with the Recall) and place his reward on the ground, but keep holding it. Show the dog the reward and give him the Sendaway command, "Away", while patting the ground where he must drop. As the dog runs out, praise him and repeat the command, and as he reaches you tell him to go down. The Down should not be a problem as the dog is next to you. Once the dog is down, praise him for a few seconds, then release him and give him his reward.

Repeat this step until the dog is going down automatically as he reaches you. At this point, you must make sure the dog is taught to take his reward only when told to do so. You must also make sure that the dog lies down in front of the reward, not to one side of it. To help him understand this, you can alternate positioning yourself to the left and the right of the reward, as the dog will have the tendency to lie opposite you if you stay in one place.

The dog has now been taught to run out on command and to drop when told to do so, which is, in fact, exactly what he must do in competition. All that is left to do is to re-position yourself at the starting point. However, before doing this, you can introduce the most valuable command in the whole exercise – the command "Look straight". If you can convince the dog that his reward is always straight in front of his nose, then you will get good Sendaways. So, before going on to the next step, introduce the Look straight command while the dog is already looking straight.

Once you have taught Step One, and the dog understands what is required, you can sit the dog, walk out to the dropping point and place his reward on the ground. As the dog looks at the reward, in anticipation of being called, you can introduce the "Look straight" command before calling the dog. It is important to introduce the command only while the dog is looking straight. It is the same principle of giving a name to a particular activity while the dog is already doing what we require of him. If the dog occasionally looks away, just give him the Sendaway command. However, if the dog habitually looks away, then take a good look at his motivation and how much he wants his reward.

Certain dogs have the tendency to run out in a curve in this step. If this happens, you can shorten the distance to the point where the dog stops curving and runs straight, and then gradually build up the distance to the required point. Alternatively, you can teach the dog to run through parallel tapes, which will eliminate the opportunity of curving. Both methods will help, if taught carefully and gradually.

STEP TWO

Once Step One has been taught satisfactorily, you can proceed to sending the dog instead of calling him. Start off by repeating the previous step, two or three times. Then, as the dog runs in, instead of releasing him take him gently by the collar, run him back to the starting point and point him in the direction of his reward. If he understands and looks in the direction of the reward, tell him to "Look straight", and then give him the Sendaway command. As he runs out, walk out behind him and drop him as he reaches his reward. If the dog does not look towards the reward, do not send him, but run out with him while holding his collar and let him have the reward. It is important that you always follow the dog out. There is no point in standing still and shouting at your dog from a distance. If the dog believes that you are always just behind him, he will drop quickly on command, but if he learns that you are some distance away and that you have little or no control over him, you will create problems.

At this stage, you will have to adapt your training depending on whether you are using food or toy as reward. If you are using a toy, then the dog should have been previously taught to leave and take on command. If this has not been taught, it must be done before proceeding further. The aim is to send the dog to his toy and drop him before he picks up his toy, which he may only do on command. If you have to start shouting at the dog to leave his toy, you will be defeating the object of the lesson. If taught correctly, the dog will run out and go down on command without touching the toy. He will look to you for the command to take the toy, which only comes after he has gone down. The dog will then learn that the quicker he obeys the Down command, the sooner he can have his toy, which is just what you want. When using food as the reward, you will have to adapt the timing of the reward, and will need to use two pieces of food to reward the dog. The first piece is placed at the dropping point and the dog will be allowed to eat this before getting the command to drop. You will have to walk out after the dog, and the second piece of food is given from the hand after the dog has carried out the command to drop. The Down command should not be given until the dog has finished eating the first piece, because this will create a slow Down. The dog will learn to run out for the first reward, and then go down quickly to obtain the second reward. In the ring, when the first reward is not available, the dog, on hearing the command "Down" will look to the handler for the second reward.

With both food or toy rewards, you will know the dog understands this step when you see him reaching his reward and then going down in order to get the Take it command for his toy, or going down after eating his first food reward in order to get the second reward. Once this is happening, you can proceed further.

STEP THREE

Up until now, the dog has always been shown where his reward was prior to being sent. In Step Three, the dog must learn that he must trust you, because you always *know* where his reward is. To do this, let the dog do two or three Sendaways as per Steps One and Two. Then, leave the reward in the same place and take the dog out of the training area completely for a minute or two. Bring the dog back in to the start point, and line him up for the Sendaway. Encourage the dog to "Look straight", and if you see that he understands,

Encourage the dog to "Look straight" when setting up for the Sendaway exercise.

send him, and finish off the exercise as per Step Two. If the dog looks confused or hesitant, just give him the Away command and run him out on the lead to his reward.

All we want to achieve in this step is to develop the dog's belief that we *know* where his reward is. To do this, gradually increase the time period between showing the dog his reward and actually sending him to the point where you have placed his reward, and then do all the other exercises before actually sending him.

STEP FOUR

Leave the dog in the house or car, and place his reward at the end of the Sendaway area. Bring the dog into the area and set him up for the Sendaway. At this point the dog has not seen you place his reward, so this will test his ability to trust that you know where his reward is. As in the previous step, your ability to read the dog and see if he understands will be the deciding factor in sending him or running him out. This step should be simple and straightforward as the dog has already been sent to the same point many times in the previous steps, and he should now be confident that you know where his reward is. As in all Sendaway training, follow the dog out to ensure a fast Down, and reward as per food or toy.

STEP FIVE

At this stage, you have taught the dog to do a fast, correct Sendaway from one point to another, always using the same starting and finishing point. We must now increase the dog's experience by choosing another area and repeating the basic steps. Once that has been done, choose another area and so on until the dog is confident and happy to be sent to several different places. If possible, try to choose a different area each time. If your training area is restricted, then you can use the same area twice, but always send the dog in the opposite direction. Never try to send an inexperienced dog to a new drop if a point, previously used, is within his field of vision.

STEP SIX

You can now begin to introduce markers to the Sendaway. When first introducing markers it is worthwhile placing the dog on the lead and teaching him to walk (not Heelwork) through the markers. If the dog wants to sniff the markers, let him do so; he must be confident that they are not dangerous. Once he has inspected them and sees that they are pretty boring things, we can place them as Sendaway markers. At first they should be placed just in front of the dog at the starting point, and once the dog is running through and ignoring them, they can be gradually moved further away from the starting point and nearer to the dropping point.

I believe that there is far too much fuss made of Sendaway markers. They have nothing to do with the dog's Sendaway; the dog should be taught the Sendaway without markers and should find them of no importance. I never use a back marker in training, as this will only teach the dog that a marker *can* be interesting. If the dog understands that his reward is always there, even though he cannot see it and that it is never near a marker, then markers are of no importance to the dog.

THE RECALL

Teaching the Recall is actually unnecessary, as this is a Test A Recall and has, therefore already been taught (see Chapter Eight: Teaching Recalls). When getting ready for competition, it is worthwhile to *occasionally* combine the Sendaway with a Recall. When doing this, I send the dog and then walk up to the dog and circle him (as we do with the Stay exercises) before calling the dog to Heel. This, if habitually done, will prevent anticipation of the Recall.

When using food as reward, the second reward must still be given for the drop, and a third for the Recall. If you use toys and the dog occasionally brings the toy with him when called, just ignore it. If it happens every time, then retrain the Leave and Take commands. Do not start shouting at the dog for taking the toy as this will only inhibit his Recall.

Chapter Twelve

SCENT DISCRIMINATION

A good Novice Recall is an integral part of the Retrieve exercise and, likewise, a correct Retrieve is the basis of a good Scent. If a dog has not been taught to retrieve he can still be introduced to the Scent exercise in the same way that a puppy learns to use his nose (see Chapter One: Puppy Training). However, the Retrieve exercise must be taught before the formal Scent exercise can be started.

Up until several years ago in Test A, the dog had to find the handler's article which had been placed between up to ten other articles. This meant that the dog was searching for a known article between other different, unknown articles. The current rules insist that the dog finds the handler's scent on a cloth placed between five other neutral cloths. This has resulted in many handlers teaching Scent Discrimination on cloths only, and I believe that this is the cause of many of the Scent problems that we see in competition today.

CHANNELLING THE INSTINCT

All dogs have the ability to discriminate and recognise a particular Scent. Try throwing a stick for a dog while out for a walk. It would not matter how many other sticks were lying around, the dog will always, and without any apparent effort, return with the stick that has been thrown. Why then do we have Scent failures in the ring?

A dog's ability to discriminate by smell is far greater than that of humans. In the Scent exercise, you are asking the dog to do something that you cannot do yourself. You do not (and cannot) teach the dog how to discriminate, this is an inborn, natural ability. Your task is to teach the dog to find the scent that you want him to find, on your command. All you will be doing is channelling this natural ability into a formal exercise. By creating a situation where the dog cannot go wrong and is then praised for being correct, you will end up with a happy, confident dog.

I use two different methods to teach Scent, one based on play reward and the other based upon food. Both methods work if they are taught properly, and with the average dog, the choice of method is left to the preference of the handler. However, I have found that the play method works better with the outgoing, confident dog, whereas the food method is better suited to the quiet, less self-assured type.

With my own dogs, Wimp and Woolie, I used the play method and both these dogs have very rarely failed Scent, and would never give up. However, Wimp tended to be chaotic in that he would rush out into the scent area and dash here and there in an effort to find 'the cloth'. Woolie does Scent in exactly the same way. Wimp loved every second of this exercise, and this keenness would often result in him covering the scent area and most of the cloths several times before hitting on the correct cloth. Actual failures were few and far between (Woolie is now nine years old and has only ever failed one Scent), but there was many a show where 'the cloth' was missed several times before discovery. When Wimp won the Championships in 1989 he worked the pattern eleven times before hitting the correct cloth, all the time with a wagging tail and loving every minute – which was more than could be said for his handler!

TACKLING PROBLEMS

Another of our dogs, Jock, trained by my wife Ria, was initially trained by the play method, but after a nasty experience during the Scent exercise (he was attacked by another Collie that was sitting on the sideline as he entered the scent area), he lost all confidence and ended up refusing to search the pattern and would, as often as not, retrieve the nearest cloth so that he could get back to his 'Mum' as soon as possible. Things got so bad that Ria thought of retiring Jock as he obviously did not enjoy doing the Scent exercise.

When you come up against a major problem such as this, it is important to go back through all that you have learned and see what may be of help in solving the problem. Ria and I had some experience in teaching dogs to track, using food as motivation. So going against all the rules (at that time), stating that you should never command the dog over the scent-articles, we started to place food on the tiles that were used in place of cloths – one piece on each tile. We were not teaching a Scent, all we wanted was to give Jock the confidence to go into the area and check out the tiles for his reward. Within a week or two, Jock was happily going back out into the scent area and his lack of confidence disappeared. I believe that if we had been 'narrow-minded' and stayed with the proven method and refused to experiment, we would never have cured this problem. Five years later our experience with Jock was used again with Kelsey, Ria's German Shepherd Dog.

Kelsey was having confidence problems with the Scent exercise. She either did not want to go out and search, or if she went, she was reluctant to use her nose. We decided to use food rewards to build up her confidence and, as with Jock, within a week or two Kelsey was happily and correctly doing a good Scent exercise.

The experiences with Jock and Kelsey reaffirmed the lesson that I always try to adhere to when confronted with a problem. I have a preferred method that works most times for most types of dog. In reserve, I have options that I have picked up over the years from watching, listening to, and being taught by many other trainers. I never reject a method just because it differs from the method I usually prefer to use. This open-mindedness allowed Ria to re-teach Jock and Kelsey when my standard method had failed. Years ago, I would have struggled on with 'my' method, just because it had been successful in the past with our other dogs.

The method I choose to teach is dictated by the dog's reaction to play. If the dog is keen to chase after a toy and will play willingly, I will, as often as not, use the play method. If the dog is not the outgoing playful type, then I will use food.

TAKING SCENT

In Class A and Class B the dog only has to find the handler's scent and, therefore, many handlers neglect to teach the dog to take scent from a cloth. This may not cause any problems until Class C, where the dog has to discriminate between the judge's scent on a cloth, and from both decoy and neutral cloths. In the lower classes, the dog has only to find the familiar scent of someone he lives with, and he would probably find this scent even if he was not given scent prior to the exercise. In training, I always give the dog my scent from a cloth, so that he is in the habit of sniffing the cloth long before Class C.

Learning to take scent. Teach the dog to hold the cloth, and loosely fold it over the nose.

Teaching a dog to sniff the cloth is very simple. Take a piece of wet food and rub the food on the palm of your hand, then cover the hand with a cloth and let the dog sniff the cloth. As he does so, quietly praise him for a second or two and then remove the cloth. Place the food in your hand, and reward the dog by giving him the food. Gradually reduce the amount of food that is rubbed on the hand until it can be completely dispensed with, and the only scent that remains on the hand is your own. Next, rub the cloth between your hands to saturate it with scent, and hold it out in front of your dog. As he sniffs the cloth, praise him and reward him. Within a few days, the dog will learn to sniff each cloth as it is held in front of him; a second or two is enough time for the dog to remember the scent.

I then teach the dog to sit with his head slightly raised and to remain still, holding the cloth by the edge between his front teeth. I then place the cloth over his nose, just hanging loosely over his nostrils. I do not hold the cloth in place on his nose, as I want as little of my scent as possible to mix with the judge's scent. I let the dog sit still for five seconds, breathing through the cloth, and then remove the cloth.

I have never understood why some people pump the dog's stomach or back end, or do other strange things to their dogs when giving scent. Many insist that their dogs refuse to take scent and this pumping makes the dog breathe. I have my doubts about this, but if it is so, I would suggest that they have a good look at the dog's attitude; he obviously does not want to do the exercise, which suggests a training fault.

PLAY METHOD

Prior to teaching the formal Scent exercise, I teach the dog to find a variety of toys, a knotted rag, and other articles hidden in various places in and around the house. The dog will also correctly retrieve these articles, if told to do so.

STEP ONE: IMMOVABLE ARTICLES

Select several large articles, such as flower pots, house bricks, old pans or such like. It does not really matter what you use, as long as the articles cannot be picked up by the dog. Wear rubber gloves or plastic bags on your hands to make sure that you do not contaminate them with your scent. If you have someone to help you lay out these articles, gloves are not necessary. It is only important that your scent is not on the articles. Place the articles in a group on the ground in an area of about four square yards.

Select an article that the dog must find, and let the dog retrieve the article a couple of times. Next, throw the article into the immovable articles and command the dog to retrieve the article from between the immovable articles. Do this several times until the dog is happily entering the scent area to pick up 'his' article. At this point, the dog will be using his eyes to find his article but this is not important. All we want is to give the dog the confidence to enter the scent area to collect his article.

Place the dog in the Sit, walk into the scent area and place his article in plain view. Then return to the dog, and send him to find his article by giving him the Retrieve command. After repeating this a couple of times, start to place the article behind one of the larger immovable articles, so that the dog cannot see it until he has entered the scent area. The dog will probably mark the place that you have dropped the article but, once again, this is not important. Repeat this once or twice, and then go out and pretend to place the article behind one of the larger articles while, in fact, it is placed behind another article. The dog will go out to where he thinks the article is, and when he finds that it is not where he thought, he will proceed to search for it. While the dog is searching for his article the Find command can be introduced. The dog will be searching with both eyes and nose but, as yet, this is irrelevant.

By the end of this phase, the dog should be happily going out into the scent area and looking for his article and then retrieving it. The moment that the dog has found his article, the Scent becomes a Retrieve and should be handled as such, with the dog being called out of the area as in teaching the Retrieve. This phase should be repeated using several different articles, including a knotted rag, until the dog will happily search for and retrieve a variety of articles. At this point, the Retrieve prior to doing Scent can be dispensed with, so that the dog does not know beforehand what he must find and will learn to use his nose to recognise the article. All scent-articles that are to be found should, however, be known to the dog.

The immovable articles can now be placed in a straight line, with the scented article placed in various places in the line. As before, you must pretend to place the article in several different places before actually dropping it, to encourage the dog to search for the article.

STEP TWO: TENTS.
By now, the dog should be happily going out into the scent area and searching for 'his' article. Until now, it has not particularly mattered if the dog has been using his nose, his eyes, or a combination of both to find his article. In this step, the dog will learn to use his nose because the articles will be hidden under tents. The tents I use are made of quarter-inch thick plastic, which is 12 ins wide by 24 ins, and folded at a right-angle across the middle to form a tent, with both ends open.

These tents are placed, one by one, over the immovable articles until all the articles are covered by a tent. The scent-article can then be placed under an empty tent out of sight of the dog, which will encourage the dog to use his nose to find it. The first couple of times it may be necessary to place the article half under the tent, to let the dog understand that he must look under the tents.

As before, let the dog see you place the article and, once he is confident, you can pretend to place the article under several different tents before actually placing it. By the end of this phase of training, the dog should be using his nose to find his article, which he cannot find by sight.

STEP THREE: CLOTHS ON TILES
Once the dog is happily searching the row of immovable articles which are under tents, you can gradually, one for one, replace the immovable articles with tiles that are encased in cloth. I prefer to use aluminium tiles, specially cut to size. The cloths are made up into envelopes that fit snugly over the tiles. I also have a smaller tile, which is placed under the scent-cloth, so that the aluminium smell is on all cloths.

Learning to find the Scent-article, which is hidden under one of the tents.

As the dog become more confident, place the tents in a straight line so that the dog works his way along, searching for the scent-article.

By replacing the immovable articles one at a time, you will end up with a row of cloths, and the dog will find his article from among this row of neutral cloths. Occasionally, I will still use a different article that the dog must find from among these cloths. I have found that if a certain type of dog always has to find a cloth among other cloths, he becomes cloth orientated. This sometimes leads to the dog picking up the neutral cloths by sight, and then rejecting them by taste and smell in the ring. Alternating the scent-article, placed between the cloths, suppresses this fault.

Gradually you can remove the tents until the dog is searching the row of neutral cloths to find his article. At this point, a scented cloth can be used as the scent-article, with the occasional 'other' article to avoid cloth obsession.

STEP FOUR: DECOYS

The time has now come to introduce a decoy into the scent pattern. Ask a helper, preferably a stranger and definitely not a family member, to lightly hold one of the tiles, encased with a cloth, for a few seconds before placing this decoy in the row. With the dog watching, place the scent-cloth with your scent on it in the row beyond the decoy cloth. Send the dog out to find the cloth. As often as not, the dog will just ignore the decoy and find your cloth. However, if he does react to the decoy, he must not be corrected. The whole principle of placing all neutral and decoy cloths on tiles is to prevent the dog from picking up the wrong cloth, without handler influence. Once the dog realises that this strange, scented cloth cannot be picked up, he will carry on and find the correct cloth.

Once the dog has learnt that the decoy cannot be picked up and is ignoring it, he can be positioned with his back to the scent area so that he cannot see where the scent-cloth is placed. You can then introduce a second, and then later, a third decoy in the same way until the dog is confidently ignoring the decoys and finding 'his' cloth containing the handler's scent. The dog is now doing a Class B Scent.

STEP FIVE: REMOVING THE TILES

When you have ascertained that the dog is capable and confident in both Class A and Class B Scents, you can remove the tiles. However, I never set out a scent pattern with cloths lying loose on the ground, which would give the dog a chance to make a mistake and pick up the wrong cloth. I use a machine, bought at the local do-it-yourself shop, to punch brass eyes into the four corners of all the scent-cloths. I then use tent pins to peg down all neutral and decoy cloths, so that the dog cannot pick up the wrong cloth. The principle is the same as when using tiles except that, with the use of tent pins, the cloths lie more naturally. The scent of the aluminium tiles is also removed.

I would *never* do a training Scent on cloths that are not tied down in this way, even with a very experienced Test C dog.

STEP SIX: TEACHING PATTERNS

Until now, the cloths have always been placed in a straight line; now the time has come to teach patterns.

Lay out a line of nine cloths, pegged down as previously described. Place the scented cloth in the line, between neutral cloths numbers eight and nine, making a row of ten cloths with the scented cloth ninth in line. Bring the dog into position at the start of the row, and command him to find his cloth. Next, place the cloth in the same position as before, position the dog at the other end of the line, with the scented cloth now second in the line, and let the dog find the cloth. Once again, place the cloth in the same place. Bring the dog to the right-hand side of the row, facing the first cloth in the row, with the row of cloths from left to right in front of the dog. The scented cloth is now off to the right. Command the dog to find. Lastly, place the dog to the left of the last cloth, which will mean that the cloths are again from left to right in front of the dog, but now the cloth is almost directly in front of him. Once again, tell the dog to find.

By putting the cloth in the same place each time and changing the starting point from where you send the dog, you have started to introduce patterns – without contaminating the ground – by constantly replacing the scented cloth. You can develop this further by imagining that the scent area is the face of a clock, with the row of cloths running from six to twelve o'clock.

By positioning the dog anywhere on the clock-face, you can introduce him to left-to-right patterns (with the dog starting from three or nine o'clock) to a diagonal or one leg of a 'V' pattern (by starting the dog from five, seven, eleven or one o'clock), or to a straight line (with the dog at six or twelve o'clock). The cloth is always in the same place.

All patterns, with the exception of a circle, will be a combination of the clock-face patterns. You can now proceed to broaden the dog's experience by systematically introducing him to various patterns, including corners to left and right, and multiple rows of cloths. I always make a sketch of all the scent patterns that I see at shows, and if I come across one that I do not know, I use that pattern the next time I train Scent.

FOOD METHOD

At one time, I believed that using food to teach Scent Discrimination would distract the dog from the job at hand. I also thought that the handler should never command the dog over the scent area. With hindsight, I realise that I was guilty of just imitating more experienced trainers and was not thinking for myself. I now realise that no one method will suit every dog or handler.

The basic technique used in food-training Scent Discrimination originates from teaching tracking dogs to follow a track. As most of us have to train alone without the help of an assistant, you must take great care not to contaminate the neutral cloths with your own scent. I prefer to use both tweezers and plastic gloves when handling the neutral cloths. I buy the disposable type of gloves that are thrown away after being used once. I also keep all clean cloths in air-tight, plastic containers, and have about twenty different containers each holding about thirty cloths. I rotate the use of these containers, so that freshly washed cloths may lie untouched as long as possible before being used. When possible, I get someone else to wash the cloths.

When employing the food method, I use a teaspoon to place the food on the cloths to avoid inadvertently touching the neutral cloths. Wherever possible, I train Scent with the help of an assistant, so that accidental contamination of the cloths is avoided.

Using the food method, the dog works along the line of cloths.

STEP ONE: COVERING ALL THE CLOTHS

With the dog watching, lay out a row of ten tiles, covered with cloths, as used in the play method. Place a small piece of food on each cloth and then, with the dog on the lead, bring him up to the first cloth and show him the food. Once the dog has eaten the food, encourage him to go to the next cloth, then the third, and so on, until he has worked the row and eaten the food from each cloth. At the end of the row, take a step or two backwards, call the dog to you and give him a food reward from the hand.

Occasionally, a dog will get to the end of the row, and then try to work back along the line of cloths to see if he has missed anything. If this happens, do not interfere, as the dog will not receive a reward, and so he will soon learn that this is pointless. The dog will soon get the idea, and you can then reduce your influence by walking a step or two behind the dog as he works the line. If the dog skips a tile, bend down and remove the food, so that the dog will not be rewarded if he turns back to cloths that he has already covered. This step can be repeated four or five times before finishing the first training session.

All that we want to achieve in this first session is to teach the dog to want to investigate each cloth for the reward. The cloth as such is not interesting, just the reward placed on it.

STEP TWO: INTRODUCING THE SCENTED CLOTH

In this step, you are going to teach the dog to recognise and retrieve a cloth that contains

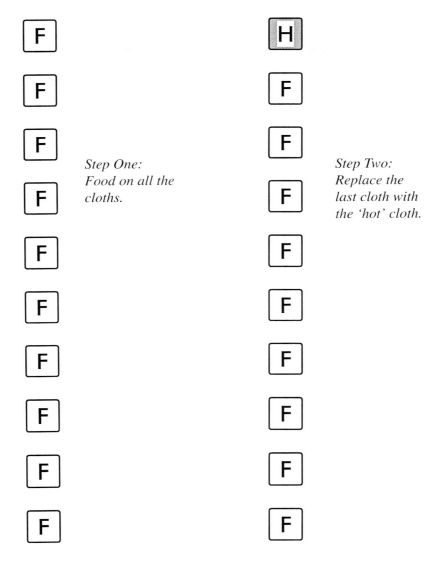

Step One:
Food on all the
cloths.

Step Two:
Replace the
last cloth with
the 'hot' cloth.

Scent Discrimination legend (for all diagrams).

*Neutral
unscented cloth
containing food*

*Handler's
'hot' scented
cloth*

*Scented decoy
cloth. All decoys
must contain food*

*Neutral
unscented cloth
without food*

your scent. The dog will receive a food reward for doing this, and, therefore, you should have food in your pocket that can be taken out and held in the hand, once the dog has started to work the row. The dog should already have been taught to retrieve a cloth, and to hold the cloth while food is held in plain view in front of his nose. This step cannot be attempted if the dog will not happily hold a cloth under the distraction of food.

Lay out a row of cloths, as in Step One, and add another cloth (without a tile) with your scent on it to the end of the row. With the dog on the lead, work the row just as in the previous step, and as the dog reaches the scented cloth, give him the command to hold. As the dog picks up the cloth, take a step or two back and encourage him to come to you by showing him the food reward in your hand. Do not demand a Present, just take the cloth and give the reward. Keep repeating this step until the dog automatically picks up the cloth without the Hold command, but always be ready to give the command at the first sign of hesitation.

The dog must be taught that the moment he finds the scented cloth the next food reward will come from your hand. Once he realises this, he will immediately pick up the scented cloth and return for the next reward. The dog can now be allowed to repeat this step off lead.

Do not attempt to go on to the next step until the dog is routinely working every neutral cloth and then immediately, and without any hesitation, picking up the scented cloth and quickly turning to the handler for the next reward, having lost all interest in the row of cloths.

STEP THREE: CHANGING THE POSITION OF THE SCENTED CLOTH

By now, the dog should be happily going out and systematically working the row of cloths until he reaches the scented cloth. He will immediately pick this up, without command, and return to the handler. You can now re-position the scented cloth so that it is no longer the last in line.

Lay out a row of tiles encased in neutral cloths that are clean and have been washed, so that there is no smell of food on them. Leave a space between cloths seven and eight, so that the scented cloth will become number eight in the row. Place food on all the neutral cloths from one to seven. No food must be placed after cloth number eight, which is the scented cloth. Bring the dog into position, and just before the first cloth, give him the Find command. Do not command the dog when he reaches the scented cloth; he will then do one of two things:

1. He will pick up the scented cloth, as he has been taught to do, and return to the handler to receive the next reward, or...

2. He will sniff the scented cloth and then carry on up the line to sniff the other neutral cloths.

Both reactions are acceptable at this stage. If the dog 'ignores' the scented cloth and carries on to the next neutral cloths he will not be rewarded, and so he will soon learn that after finding the scented cloth there are no more food rewards on the cloths. He already

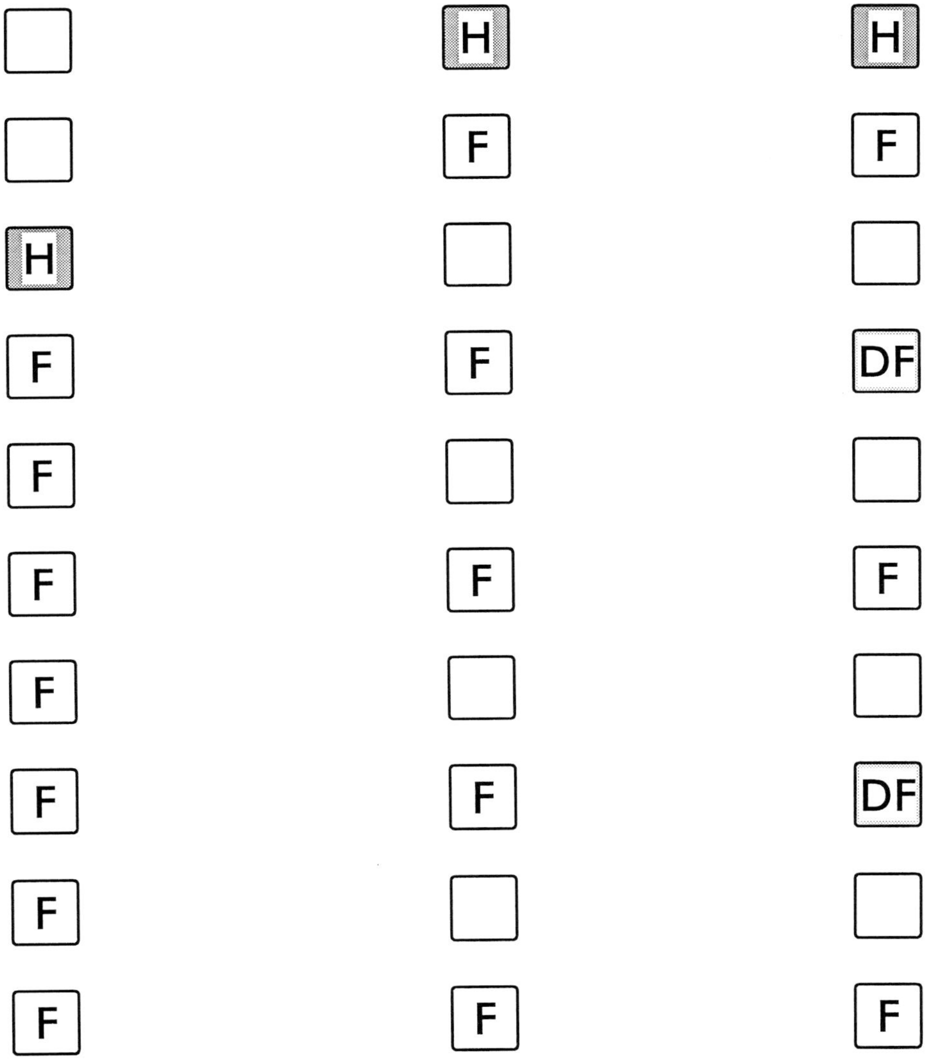

	H	H
	F	F
H		
F	F	DF
F		
F	F	F
F		
F	F	DF
F		
F	F	F

Step Three:
Repositioning the
handler's cloth.

Step Four:
Reducing food on
the cloths.

Step Five:
Introducing decoys,
always using food.

knows that picking up the scented cloth will bring a reward from the hand, and so he will return down the line to the scented cloth. Some types of dog will persevere and go over the scented cloth several times before getting the idea. This is acceptable and part of the learning process.

Within two or three training sessions the dog will understand that the scented cloth signals the end of food reward on the cloths. When this happens, you are ready to go a step further.

STEP FOUR: REDUCING THE FOOD REWARD

Until now, you have placed food on every neutral cloth. It is now time to start reducing the amount of cloths containing food. Start off by doing one Scent with food on all neutrals and then, one cloth at a time, reduce the amount of food used until it is only on alternate cloths, one, three, five, and so on. Then start putting food only on every third cloth until, with a very experienced dog, it is possible to dispense with the food completely. However, this is far in the future. In general, there is always some food, which is used to continually re-motivate the dog throughout his life.

There are some hard and fast rules relating to the use of food:

1. Always place food on the first cloth to ensure that the dog always starts searching at the nearest cloth, and works systematically over all the cloths.
2. Always place food on the decoys to discourage the dog from picking up the decoy.
3. Always put food in the corner cloths, so that the dog never learns to cut corners.
4. Never put food on cloths that are beyond the scented cloths. These cloths must be clean and have no smell of food on them.
5. Never put food on the scented cloth.
6. Always pick up any food from cloths that the dog has skipped so that he will never be rewarded for turning back.

STEP FIVE: DECOYS

It is now time to introduce decoys into the row. Ask a stranger to lightly scent a neutral cloth, and place this in the row at position number four or five. Make sure that there is food on the first cloth, the decoy cloth, and the cloth before the scented cloth. More food may be used, but these cloths must have food on them. Put the dog on the lead and command him to find. If he picks up the decoy, just show him the next food in the row without any reaction to his mistake.

When the dog sees the next piece of food, he will have to drop the decoy to get the food. At this point you can quietly remove the decoy from the ground and place it in your pocket. As the dog reaches the scented cloth and picks it up, he can be praised and receive his food reward from the hand. More decoys can be laid out as the dog becomes more confident, so long as there is food on each decoy.

STEP SIX: PATTERNS

You can now start to lay out different patterns and use the clock-face system as in the play method, always remembering that all cloths after the scented cloth must be clean and must

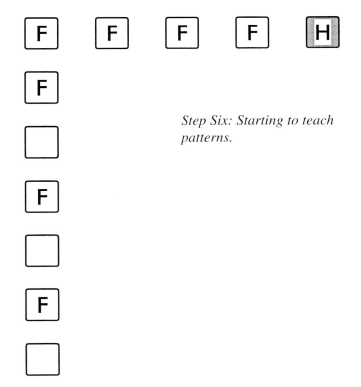

Step Six: Starting to teach patterns.

contain no food. This means that you cannot place decoys after the scented cloth. However, this will be of no consequence. A dog that is fully-trained in this method should ignore all cloths beyond the Scented cloths, and will return to the handler immediately after finding the correct cloth.

Once corners are incorporated into the scent pattern, you must remember to place food in each corner so that the dog never learns to cut corners.

No method is perfect, and there are one or two patterns that may cause the dog to retrace his steps and, therefore, be rewarded for doing so. A circle is one of these patterns, and three rows of three cloths is another. When teaching these patterns, I keep the dog on the lead and remove the food from any cloth that he has missed. When training a circle pattern, I guide the dog from six o'clock to work anti-clockwise, and place the scented article at five o'clock.

You should also bear in mind that a dog will not be penalised for covering the same cloths two or three times. However, this should not be encouraged in training.

STEP SEVEN: REMOVING THE TILES

The time has come to remove the tiles from the cloths and to teach Scent on cloths. However, in training, the cloths will always be pegged down in the same way as in the play method, to prevent the dog from being able to pick up the wrong cloth by mistake. All of the previous steps should be repeated on pegged-down cloths. In both methods, the neutral and decoy cloths must always be pegged down so that the dog can never succeed in picking up the wrong cloth by mistake.

TEST C SCENT

This is another example of how my point of view has changed over the years. At one time, I always said that Test C Scent should never be trained, and that a B Scent, (handler's scent with decoys) should suffice. While I still hold with the principle that training Test C Scent is generally unnecessary, I do believe that the occasional C Scent should be done with inexperienced dogs (who will go on to work Test C) to allow them to experience the (for some dogs) distasteful smell of perfume, cigarette smoke and such like. However, as a rule, I prefer to train B Scents, and with my older dogs that are used to the distasteful smells, I only ever train A or B Scents.

By bearing in mind that the Scent Discrimination exercise as done in competition is, in fact, a combination of three exercises: Scent, Retrieve and Novice Recall, you should be able to diagnose any fault that may appear and decide which exercise is at fault. In this way, the solution should be readily at hand.

Chapter Thirteen

DISTANT CONTROL

Distant Control is the only exercise that is exclusively a Test C exercise and is, in fact, a combination of six separate movements: Stand to Sit, Sit to Stand, Stand to Down, Down to Stand, Sit to Down, and Down to Sit. It is also an exercise where body signals and timing are critical.

When teaching the formal exercise, I use a combination of lead, body and voice commands simultaneously until the dog understands what is required of him. I then give the voice command, immediately followed by the body signal to ensure a quick response. I prefer to use voice commands in the ring. However, the rules allow either, so those of you who prefer a signal rather than voice command, should bear in mind that the timing of voice command and signal should be reversed.

I teach Distant Control in three distinct phases:

1. The preparation phase is where the dog is encouraged into the Stand, Sit and Down positions (See Chapter One: Puppy Training). This phase can be equally successful with a mature dog. However, if the dog has already been taught the Stand, Sit and Down for the Stay exercises, he may need to receive a verbal command to induce him to change position, whereas when teaching a puppy, you induce him into a position and then follow up with a command. The technique remains the same but the timing differs.

The advantage of this preparatory phase is that the dog will already know the verbal command, before the techniques to be used in the formal training phase are applied.

2. Phase Two is the period of training where the dog is taught the formal exercise, as demanded in the ring. In this phase, the technique of voice, lead and body signal to teach the dog the finished exercise is applied.

3. Phase Three is the maintenance phase, and is a combination of constantly repeating the basic techniques of Phase Two, and training the finished exercise in a situation that does not allow the dog to develop mistakes and, therefore, ensures happy, correct work.

Distant Control is one exercise that must always be trained and never practised as a formal exercise. I have found that even the most experienced dogs will develop faults very quickly, such as missing positions or forward movement, if the basics are not trained. It is natural for a dog to tuck his bottom in when moving from the Stand to the Sit, or to go through the Sit position when going from the Stand to the Down, thereby moving forward. This forward movement is natural and will always return if we practise instead of train.

TEACHING THE POSITIONS

Each position should be thoroughly taught before attempting to start on the next position; they should only be combined when all the positions have been taught. When first teaching a position, stand at the side of the dog, and then, once he understands, you can move in front of him. The next position is then taught at the side, then repeated from the front, and so on, through all six positions. Only once all six positions have been taught, can you start to move away from the dog. The technique used to teach each position will be a combination of lead, body signal, and command. These will be given simultaneously, until the dog understands, at which time the command will be given, immediately followed by the lead and body signal aids to ensure a quick response.

Tone of voice, to ensure that the dog understands each command, is extremely important. The commands should be given in three distinct tones. It is not necessary to shout the commands during training, and care should be taken when raising the voice in the ring that the commands, if given louder, do not change in tone. The commands I use are: "Sit", "Down", and "Back". I also precede the Back command with the dog's name. This helps the dog to the Stand from the Down, and continuity dictates, therefore, that it should also be used for the Stand from the Sit. However, the commands are a matter of personal preference, as is the choice between a signal rather than a verbal command. I would not advise the use of the command "Stand" in combination with "Sit", as they both begin with the letter S which could cause confusion.

I have listed the positions in the order that I prefer to teach them but, once again, this is a personal choice. However, I would advise leaving the Sit to Down position to last, as this is the one position where the dog must move forward. It is also the easiest position to teach.

SIT TO STAND

Place the dog in the Sit and twizzle into the Heel position, then make a quarter turn to the left so that you are facing the dog. All positions will be taught from this same starting point.

The lead should be held in the left hand and horizontal (a vertical lead will tell the dog to sit). There should be slight pressure on the lead to encourage backward movement. Place the right foot just in front of the dog's front paws to prevent forward movement. The left foot should be placed under the dog's stomach towards his back paws, to assist him to move backwards. However, the foot must not be used to lift the dog by brute force into the Stand. Bear in mind that the preparatory work has already taught the dog the meaning of the Stand command, and so the dog should stand on command with the foot and lead aids only ensuring that you get backward movement.

Give the command to stand, and simultaneously exert slight pressure on the lead while

Sit to Stand: The lead should be held in the left hand, and horizontal. Apply slight pressure on the lead to encourage backward movement. Give the command "Stand", sliding your left foot towards the back paws.

sliding the left foot towards the back paws. Any contact with the paws should be gentle, and no attempt should be made to lift the dog with the left foot. Very occasionally, a dog will be confused the first time this is done. If this happens, use the right hand to hold food under his chin, as in puppy training, to help him understand. However, this should be dispensed with as soon as possible.

Once the dog is in the Stand, praise him warmly but not so enthusiastically that he breaks the position. Make sure that the dog stands still for four or five seconds while being continually praised before he is released. Try to release the dog backwards so that he never associates forward movement with Distant Control. So, the command and aids for the Sit to Stand are name and verbal command, together with lead in left hand and use of the left foot.

Once the dog understands and reacts to the simultaneous commands and aids, the timing should be changed so that the command is given, followed one second later by the aids. This ensures that the dog will not confuse an aid with the command, which would result in the

Stand to Sit: Hold the lead in your left hand, and vertical. Give the Sit command, sliding your right foot towards the front paws.

dog relying and, therefore waiting for, the aids. If the dog starts to move sideways away from the left foot, you can try placing two poles joined by a piece of string next to the dog's left flank to prevent this.

When your dog is reacting well and is standing on voice command only, you can position yourself directly in front of the dog. The aids are slightly more difficult to apply from this position. However, they should now no longer be needed to help the dog to actually stand but are always applied as back-up to the verbal command.

STAND TO SIT

Place the dog in the Stand and position yourself as previously described. The lead should be held in the left hand (almost vertically with slight backward pressure), and the instep of the right foot should be used in a sliding motion towards the front paws to ensure backward movement. Any contact between the right foot and the front paws should be gentle. Do not step on the paws, just slide the right foot up to them.

The Sit command is given with simultaneous lead pressure and the right foot signal. Once the dog understands the timing, change to verbal command followed by the aids. Let the dog hold the Sit position for four or five seconds before releasing him. As before, once the dog is sitting on the verbal command, repeat this step from the front with the aids always being used as back-up. The commands and aids for the Stand to Sit are verbal command and right foot with the lead in the left hand.

DOWN TO SIT
Place the dog in the Down and stand next to him. Hold the lead in the left hand almost vertically, with slight backward pressure. With your weight on your left foot, the instep of the right foot should slide towards the dog's front paws in the same way as teaching the Sit from the Stand. The combination of lead in the left hand, and the right foot movement, will prevent forward movement and encourage a backward Sit.

Down to Sit: Showing left-hand backward pressure, and the right foot movement sliding towards the front paws.

Once the dog understands the verbal command, the exercise can be repeated from the front. As always, the timing must be altered once the dog is confident.

DOWN TO STAND

This position will show the value of combining body signals with the verbal commands because, although the dog has not as yet been taught this position, all the aids that will be used have already been taught in the previous two positions. Therefore, the dog will quickly understand what is required. To ensure backward movement, the dog will be taught to go through the Sit position to move into the Stand.

The lead should be held in the left hand, almost vertically, with slight backward pressure until the dog is in the Sit. Then lower the lead into the horizontal position as the dog moves from the Sit to the Stand. With all weight on the left foot, the right foot should slide towards the front paws to encourage the Sit. Then, as the dog sits, your weight should be transferred to the right foot. The left foot should be used to slide towards the back paws to assist with the Stand. The dog's name should be given, which will tell him to stand; the aids are helping him into the Sit, and then the verbal command, which he will hear as he sits, will tell him to stand.

None of this is new to the dog, and the Stand from the Down through the Sit should be one fluent motion. Balance is maintained by making sure that your weight is on the appropriate foot at the right time. Give the dog the command to stand, preceded by his name. Simultaneously, exert slight backward pressure on the lead while sliding the right foot towards the dog's front paws. As the dog sits, transfer your weight to the right foot and slide the left foot towards his back paws. At the same time, lower the lead, held in the left hand, to an almost horizontal position to ensure backward movement. As always, ensure that the dog maintains the Stand position for four or five seconds before releasing him.

So, the commands and aids for the Down to Stand position are: name and verbal command, right foot then left foot, with the lead in the left hand.

STAND TO DOWN

Place the dog in the Stand and turn to face him, as described. Hold the lead in the right hand and give the Down command, simultaneously placing the left foot on the lead to *gently* assist the dog in going down, front end first. The dog must not be forcibly pulled into the Down by massive foot pressure. The left foot is a guide, not a weapon. If the foot is used harshly, the dog will, as often as not, move sidewards to avoid the foot and, at best, will end up lying on one hip instead of in the lion stance. This may result in weeks of gentle remedial training to repair the damage. The dog should already have been taught how to go down in the preparatory training and, therefore, should need only the slightest foot pressure. Ensure that the dog stays in the Down position for the required four or five seconds before releasing him.

As before, this step should be repeated from the front once the dog understands and reacts to the verbal command. Occasionally, a dog will go down correctly while the handler is at his side, but then will go through the Sit into the Down when this is attempted from the front. This is often caused by the dog having sat so many times in other exercises while in

Stand to Down: Hold the lead in the right hand, and give the Down command, while gently placing the left foot on the lead to assist the dog to go into the Down.

the Present. Another reason is that the dog is looking up at the handler, and, therefore, the Sit is so much easier. If this fault appears, then you can re-teach the backward Down by placing both hands as a harness on the dog's shoulders, either side of his neck, while bending at the knees to encourage backward movement. Once the dog gets the idea, you can revert to the previous method using the left foot.

SIT TO DOWN
This is the only position where forward movement is unavoidable, and so the dog is allowed to move as he would naturally. This position, therefore, needs little teaching. The aids are applied to ensure instant response rather than influencing how the movement is made. The aids used are the same as for teaching the Down from the Stand. As with all the positions, the timing of command and aids is altered as the dog gains confidence.

Sit to Down: Use the same aids as for the Stand to Down. This is the only position where forward movement is unavoidable.

I train this position less than the other five because the dog is allowed to go down naturally. I also do not want to encourage forward movement.

INCREASING SPEED

When first teaching the exercise, it is important to get your priorities right. This should be firstly correct movement from one position to the next, and secondly, positive but calm commands (to teach the dog what is required). Once the dog understands and is confident, you can speed things up so that the end result is instant response to your commands. However, this should be done gradually, once the dog knows the exercises.

BUILDING UP DISTANCES

When the dog is competent and confident in all the positions, in both the Heel position and from in front, you can start to move away from the dog, one yard, and one position at a time.

Let us take the Sit to Stand as an example. Place the dog in the Sit and give him the Control command. Take two steps forward and turn to face the dog. Give the Stand command, immediately followed by the appropriate body signal (which for this position is sliding the instep of the right foot forward to discourage forward movement, and following through with the left foot, which is the signal for the dog to stand). Praise the dog for standing and return to the Heel position, praise again, and then release backwards. Repeat this step a few times and then end the training session.

Do not try any other positions in the same training session. It is far better to concentrate on one position at a time, gradually building up the distance to about fifteen paces. Once the dog is confident with one position, the next position can be taught in the same way until the dog can do all six positions at a distance. Always return to the dog and praise, then release him after each correct movement.

A common fault is combining the positions before the dog is ready, carrying on until the dog goes wrong, and then going back to the dog to correct him. This often results in the dog moving as the handler returns, because he thinks that he has made a mistake. By returning to the dog to praise and release him after each position, you can avoid this mistake.

COMBINING THE POSITIONS
The rules for competition state that the dog must be left in either the Stand, Sit or Down position, and then has to be given six commands from a distance of not less than ten feet.

Our training to date has taught the dog the six possible movements, one at a time, as separate exercises. It is now time to start combining the movements into the formal exercise. However, the transition from the movements as single exercises to multiple combinations of the same must be carried out gradually, starting with two commands, then three, and so on, until the goal is reached.

Place the dog in a position, give the Control command and take a step or two forward, then turn and face the dog. Praise the dog to encourage him, then give him the command for another position, praise, return to him and praise him again, but do not release him. Instead, repeat the Control command and, once again, leave and face the dog from a step or two away. Give the dog another command, and return to praise and release him.

You have now combined two positions for the first time. Now you can try three positions, remembering to return to the dog after each command to give the dog confidence. Gradually increase the distance while, at the same time, varying the number of positions given – sometimes only one, the next time three, another time five, then back to one, so that the dog gains confidence. As the dog gains experience, you can give a position, then praise the dog from a distance without returning to him, and then give him a second command.

By constantly varying the number of commands given, the distance at which they are given, and the amount of times you return to praise the dog between commands, you can avoid the most common faults of missed positions and forward movement. At the same time, you should remember to constantly repeat the basic exercise at Heel or immediately in front of the dog to maintain speed and ensure correct movements.

NATURAL BARRIERS

I often see handlers training Distant Control behind a line, and correcting the dog if he dares to put a foot over this line. I believe that this causes inhibition and hesitation in a dog, and so I advise against it. However, there are several natural barriers that can be used which will prevent forward movement without causing inhibition.

Our dogs love travelling in the car and have been taught as puppies not to jump out of the car unless told to do so. This makes the back of the car an ideal natural barrier, and it is my training place for teaching Distant Control at a distance. Obviously, this only works because our dogs have already been taught that they must not jump out of the car without permission. It would be wrong to attempt to train DC in the back of a car and then to correct the dog for jumping out, if he has never been taught not to do so.

Another natural barrier are stairs. I place my dog at the bottom of the stairs and myself at the top for the upward positions – Down to Sit, Sit to Stand and Down to Stand. I then reverse things with the dog at the top of the stairs for the downward positions – Stand to Sit, Stand to Down and Sit to Down. With a little imagination, this principle can be applied to many situations. Any barrier that prevents forward movement without instilling fear can be used.

It will now be obvious that teaching Distant Control with a combination of voice, body and lead signals, as described, demands a certain amount of expertise from the handler. I have found that practising the movements for each position, without a dog, in front of a mirror helps to develop the necessary co-ordination. Once this has been done, I then ask a friend who understands the method to act as 'dog' and to tell me which position I am giving with the body signals and lead (tied to a kitchen chair). If I confuse the friend, I will most certainly confuse the dog. In this way, the method can be perfected before attempting to teach the dog.

In competition, as often as not, the handler is given a card with the sequence of commands written on it prior to starting the exercise. I often use a small plastic box with a white lid to simulate this card. The box contains the food rewards, and this helps to keep the dog's attention. However, some judges prefer to dispense with the card and ask the stewards to give the commands to the handler. Therefore, the dog should also be taught to do the exercise while your hands are held naturally at your sides.

Although Distant Control is a Test C only exercise, I believe that it should be taught to puppies, and each phase of training should be slowly and carefully taught to the dog. It is an exercise that can take many months to perfect. The Distant Control exercise should also be perfected before an attempt is made to teach the advanced positions, as the DC commands are also used in teaching the Advanced Stand, Sit and Down.

Chapter Fourteen

PREPARING TO SHOW

Once your dog is becoming more advanced in training, he can be entered for a show, and you can start preparations for competing. Experienced competitors who are training a second or a third dog will have already developed a method of preparation. However, for the novice handler, the traumatic experience of entering a show is still to come. Many handlers compare competing to a visit to the dentist! There is no substitute for experience, but there are ways of preparing for a show that will help.

PRIOR TO THE DAY OF THE SHOW

WORKING A ROUND WITHOUT A DOG
Once a handler has learnt footwork and correct deportment, a training ring can be set up with a judge and a steward. The steward should carry out all the competition protocol, telling the competitor which exercise to do, where to stand, and so on. The handler can then complete a novice round, applying all the aids, with his imaginary dog. At the end of the round, the judge can offer advice. In this way, a novice handler can at least practise working under commands from a steward in a ring environment.

WORKING A ROUND WITH A DOG
After working the round without a dog several times, the handler can attempt the same round with the same Heelwork pattern, with commands being given by the same steward. However, just because the steward is giving commands, this does not mean that the handler has to listen to them. You can, if you wish, ignore the commands if you do not not feel confident, and turn when you want. The steward can assist by forewarning the handler which turn is coming by saying: "About-turn coming ... About-turn", and so on. This gives the handler time to prepare for the turn.

CASSETTE PLAYERS AND WALKMANS
If a steward is unavailable, a similar situation can be created by using a Walkman or a cassette player. The Walkman will allow the handler to learn to turn on command, without

disturbing the dog, whereas the cassette player will allow both dog and handler to hear and get used to the commands.

AT THE SHOW

LEARNING AND PRACTISING THE ROUND
Many experienced handlers prefer not to learn the Heelwork round before entering the ring. However, I find that I work better if I know which turn is coming. Novice handlers should learn and even practise the round, without the dog, before entering the ring. We all know the feeling of approaching the ropes and knowing that a turn is coming, but not which one. This can be very upsetting for a nervous beginner, causing hesitation which will be transferred to the dog. Nervousness will not be eradicated, but it can be controlled.

WARMING UP
A certain amount of warming up is advisable prior to entering the ring. However, it should not be over-done. The dog will not learn anything in the half-hour prior to competing that he does not already know. Some dogs will be upset if the warming up is in any way different from a normal training session. As most handlers are nervous before competing, it is very difficult to react in the same way as we do in training.

I prefer to warm the dog up by training all the exercises that he loves, thereby building his confidence, rather than training his weak exercises, which may entail having to correct him. As often as not, the warming up is for the handler's benefit, so if you cannot keep your nerves under control and be positive and friendly, it may be better not to warm up the dog at all.

IN THE RING
If the dog has been taught to pay absolute attention, he will notice the slightest difference in your body language, and this is the most common cause of dogs 'failing' in the ring. If this happens, it is better to ask the judge if you can continue with a training round, and then apply all the aids in the same way as in training at home.

A training round is not an opportunity to pull and moan at the dog. If the dog is not paying attention, his name (which is also the attention-getting command) should be called out in a firm tone of voice, but without inducing fear. In the lower classes, this would not even be marked, as extra commands are permitted.

One of the most difficult parts of competing is recapturing exactly the same attitude and tone of voice, and applying the aids in the same way under the stress of competing as we do in training. Always bear in mind that if the handler acts differently, the dog will react to the difference.

AFTER COMPETING
Most often handlers come out of the ring with a feeling of dissatisfaction or disappointment. This is something that you must learn to cope with, as rounds that give satisfaction are few and far between. If things have gone wrong in the ring, try and put the experience into

perspective – and do not take it out on the dog. So many handlers swear that their dogs purposely make mistakes, or do things their own way. Comments such as: "he knows I won't correct him in the ring", or other such ridiculous remarks are often heard in the showground. If you take credit for the dog's successes, you should also take responsibility for his failures. After all, it *is* only a hobby.